THE *Slanted* LIFE of

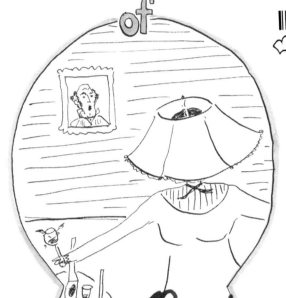

Emily Dickinson

AMERICA'S FAVORITE RECLUSE JUST GOT A LIFE!

HOW TO THROW A PARTY

as imagined by
ROSANNA BRUNO

Andrews McMeel
Publishing®
a division of Andrews McMeel Universal

FOR ROSEMARY LEONE, MARIETTA AGOCS, DENNIS HAUGH,
ROSEMARY NAAB, MARIA RAFFAELE, NANCY HILL,
AND FRAN CARDAMONE. THANKS FOR LETTING ME IN
THE SECOND FLOOR FACULTY ROOM!

Contents

THE Slanted LIFE of Emily Dickinson

INTRODUCTION

Emily Dickinson's celebrity status can be attributed as much to her life (or supposed lack of one) as to the thousands of poems she composed.

My introduction to Dickinson was (way back) in high school. I was floored by the immediacy of her voice and her unusual use of language. But I was impressed by the myth surrounding her life and found it somewhat comical. Did she only wear white? Was she a total recluse? Did she have a love life? Was she obsessed with death? So much emphasis has been placed on the poet's persona and the myth of her life that I could not help but imagine a more slanted version. So, as any (amateur) scholar would do, I looked to the poems for answers. Using Emily's own words, it is with obsessive reverence and extreme nerdiness that I present the poet as someone who enjoys clicking around on Facebook, Twitter, and Instagram. She is someone who may throw wild parties, play poker, or appear on reality tv.

Dickinson said: "Tell all the truth but tell it slant." I do just that in the pages of this book. Here is an Emily Dickinson for the 21st century.

~ Rosanna Bruno

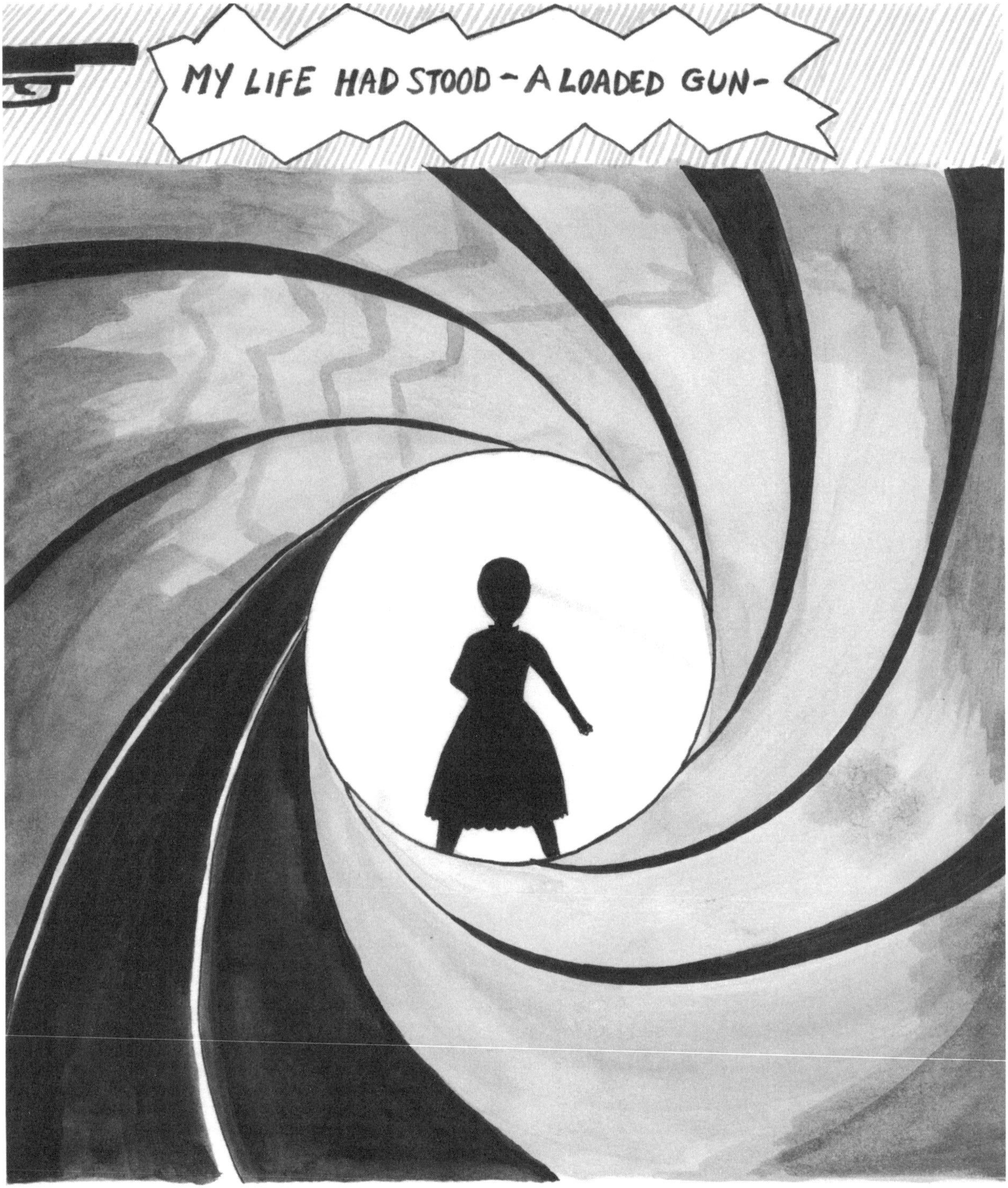
MY LIFE HAD STOOD - A LOADED GUN-

DICKINSON, EMILY DICKINSON

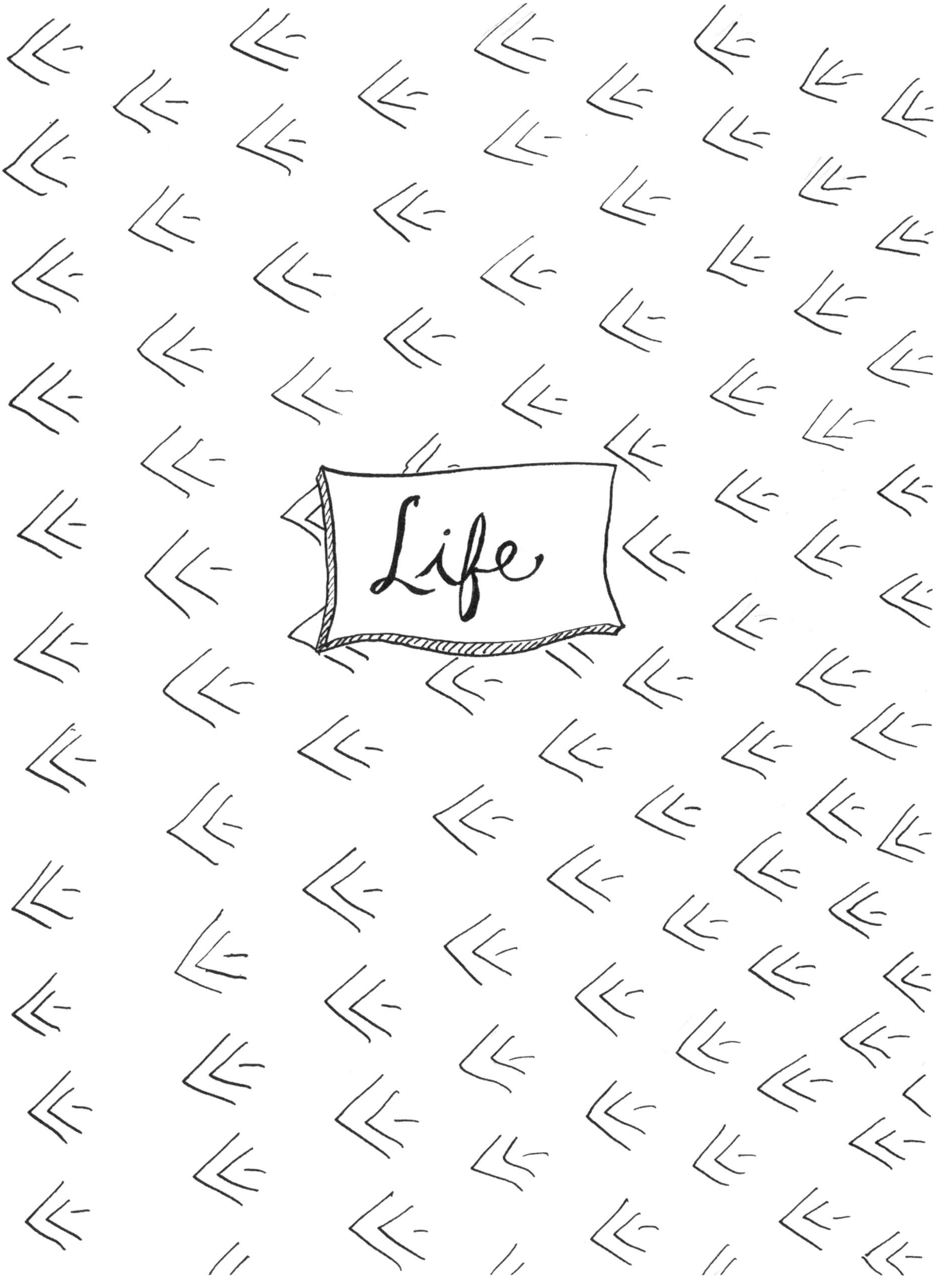
Life

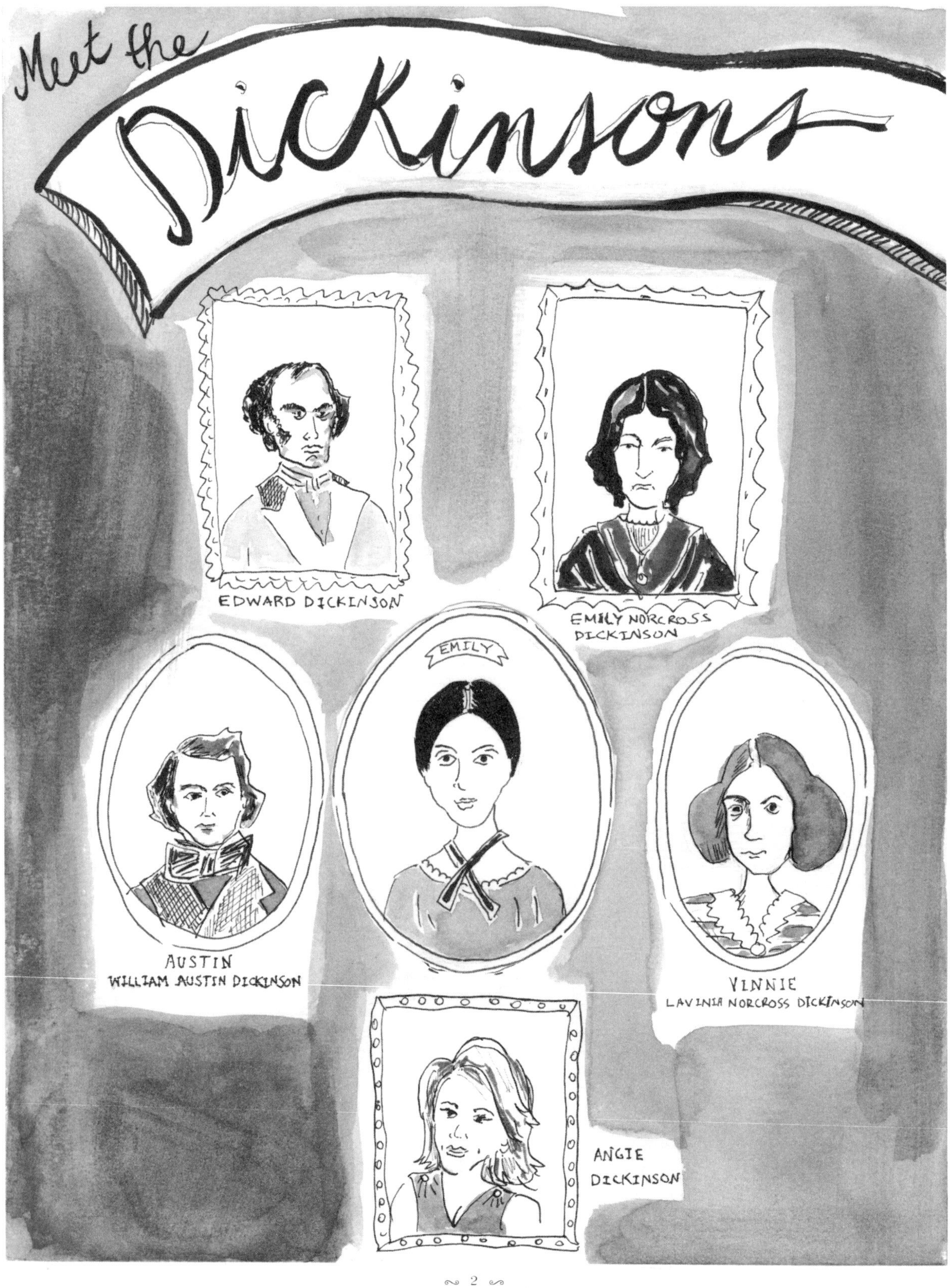

Meet the
Dickinsons
EDWARD DICKINSON
EMILY NORCROSS
DICKINSON
EMILY
AUSTIN
WILLIAM AUSTIN DICKINSON
VINNIE
LAVINIA NORCROSS DICKINSON
ANGIE
DICKINSON

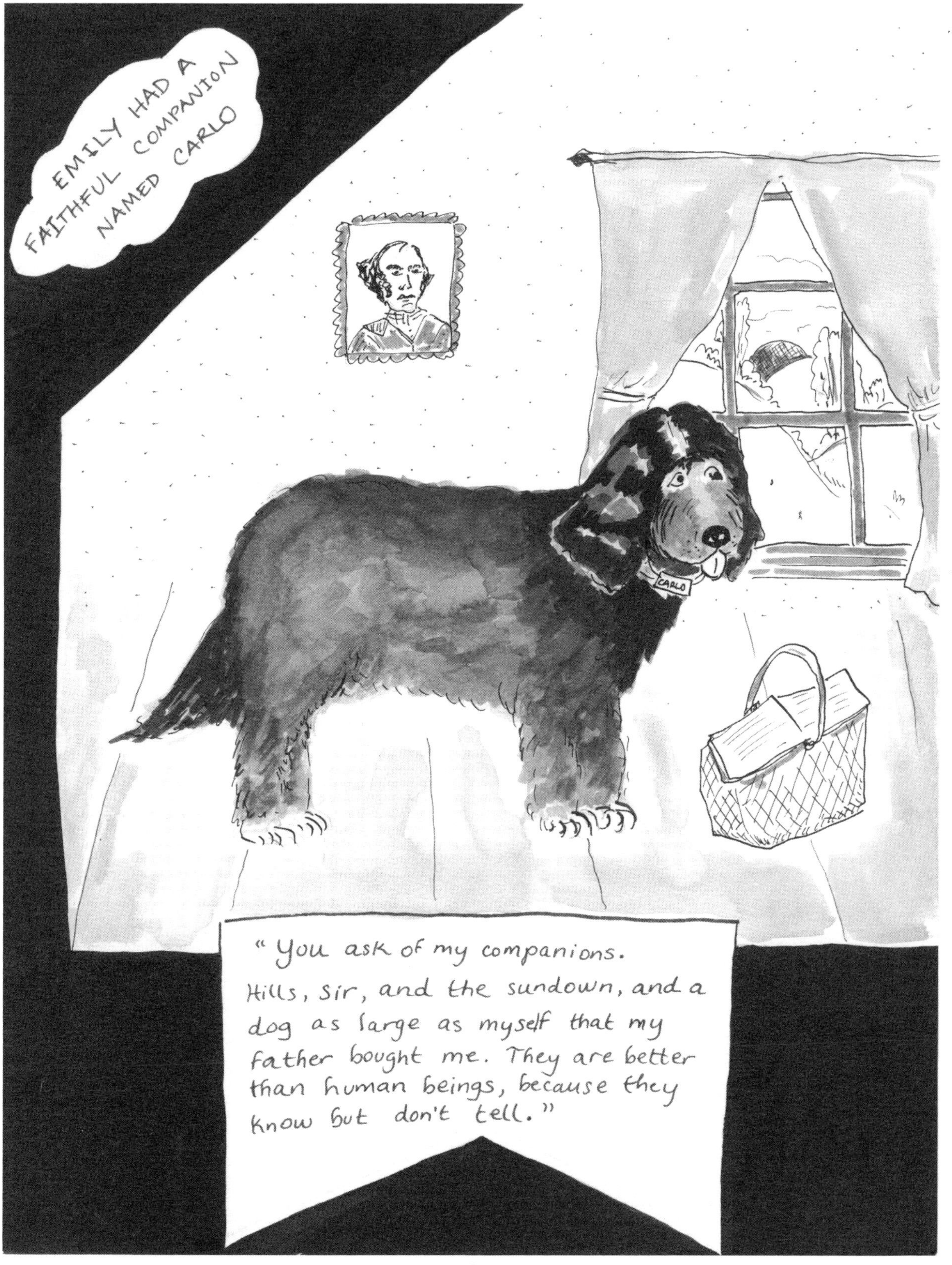
EMILY HAD A FAITHFUL COMPANION NAMED CARLO
CARLO
“You ask of my companions. Hills, sir, and the sundown, and a dog as large as myself that my father bought me. They are better than human beings, because they know but don't tell.”

A Poet's Beginnings PART 1

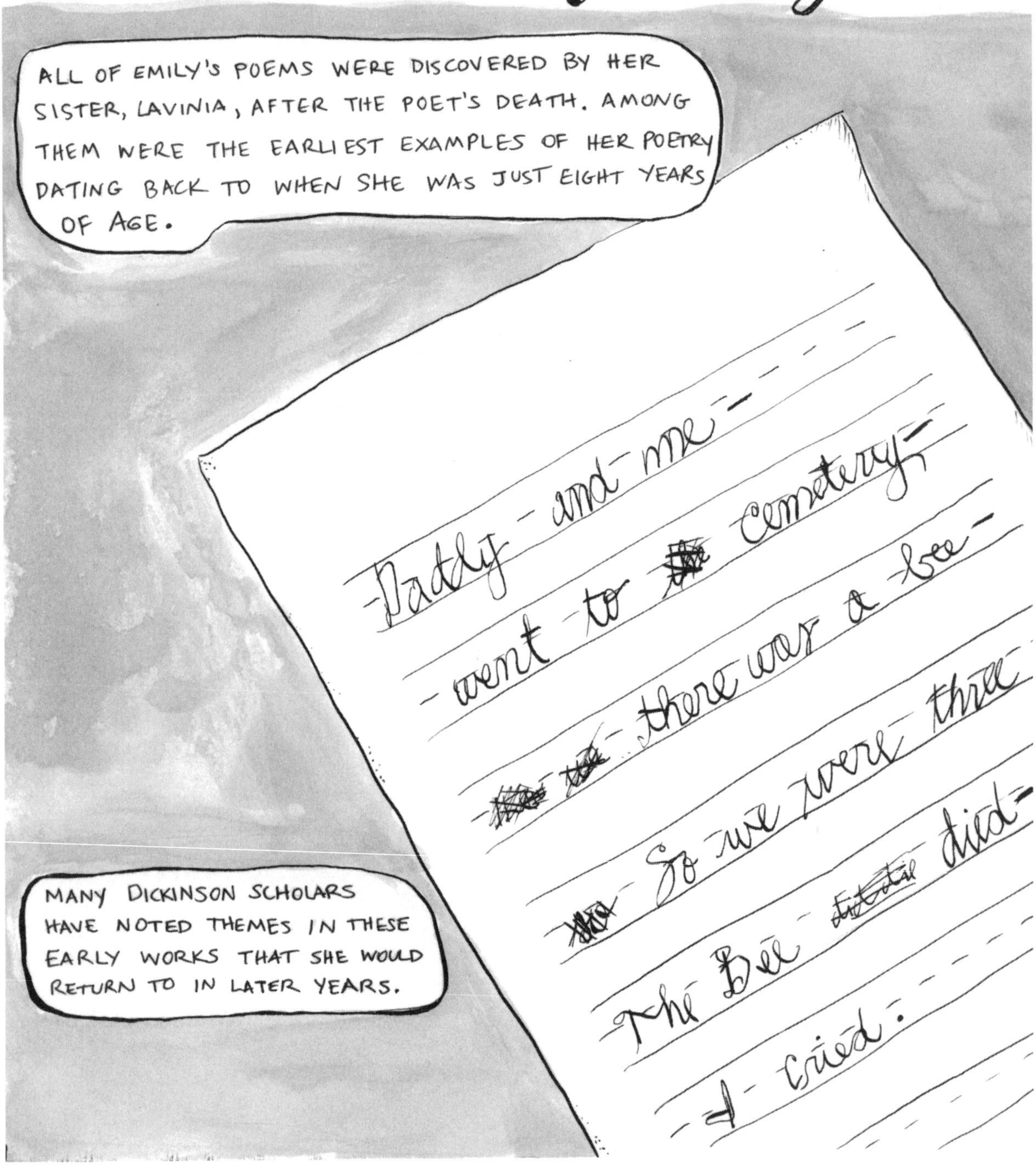

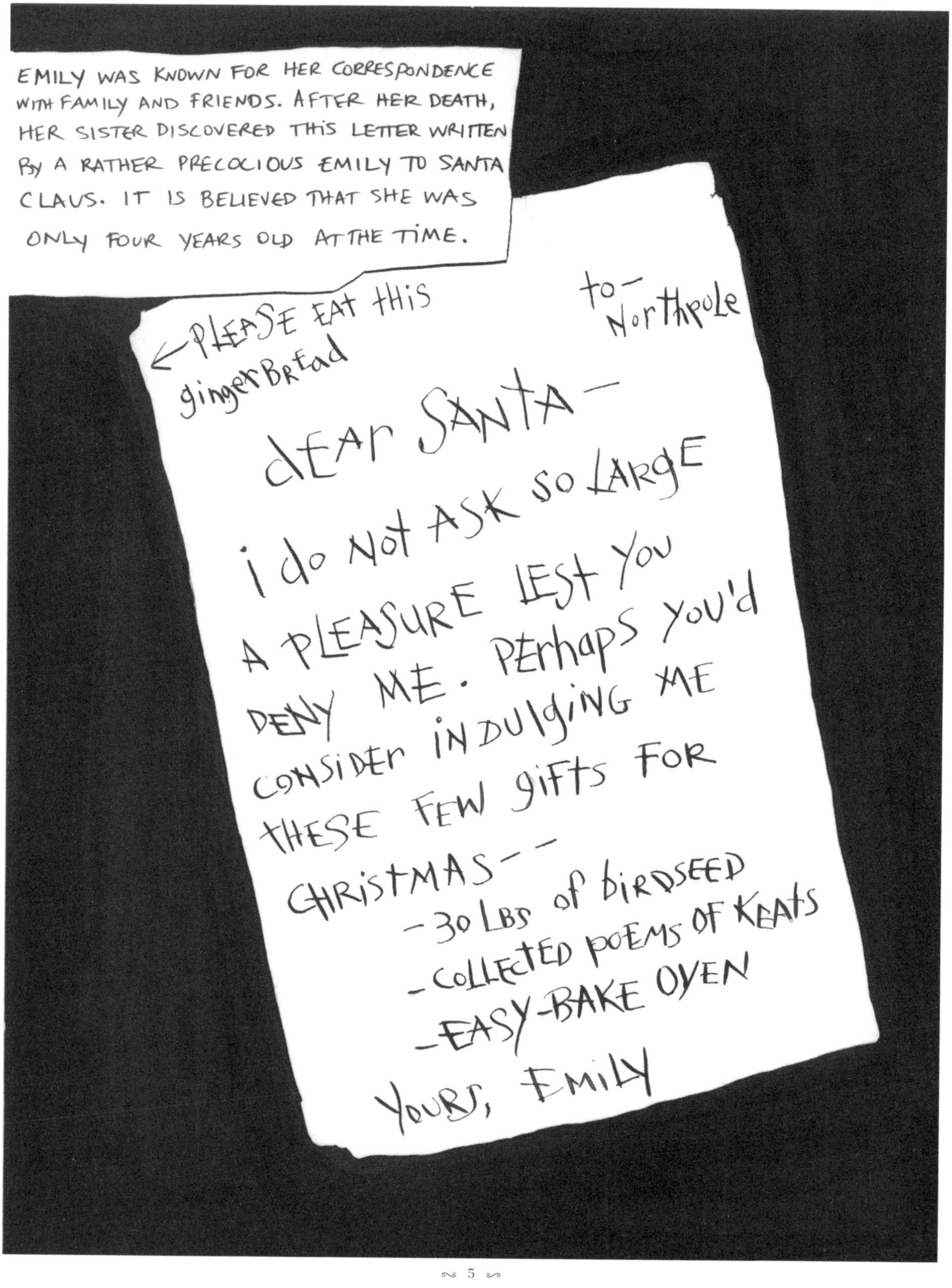
EMILY WAS KNOWN FOR HER CORRESPONDENCE WITH FAMILY AND FRIENDS. AFTER HER DEATH, HER SISTER DISCOVERED THIS LETTER WRITTEN BY A RATHER PRECOCIOUS EMILY TO SANTA CLAUS. IT IS BELIEVED THAT SHE WAS ONLY FOUR YEARS OLD AT THE TIME.
← PLEASE EAT THIS gingerBread
to— Northpole
dear SANTA—
i do Not ASK SO LARGE A PLEASURE LEST YOU DENY ME. PErhaps you'd CONSIDER INDULGING ME THESE FEW gifts FOR CHRISTMAS——
- 30 LBS of BIRDSEED
- COLLECTED POEMS OF KEATS
- EASY-BAKE OVEN
YOURS, EMILY

A Poet's Beginnings PART 2

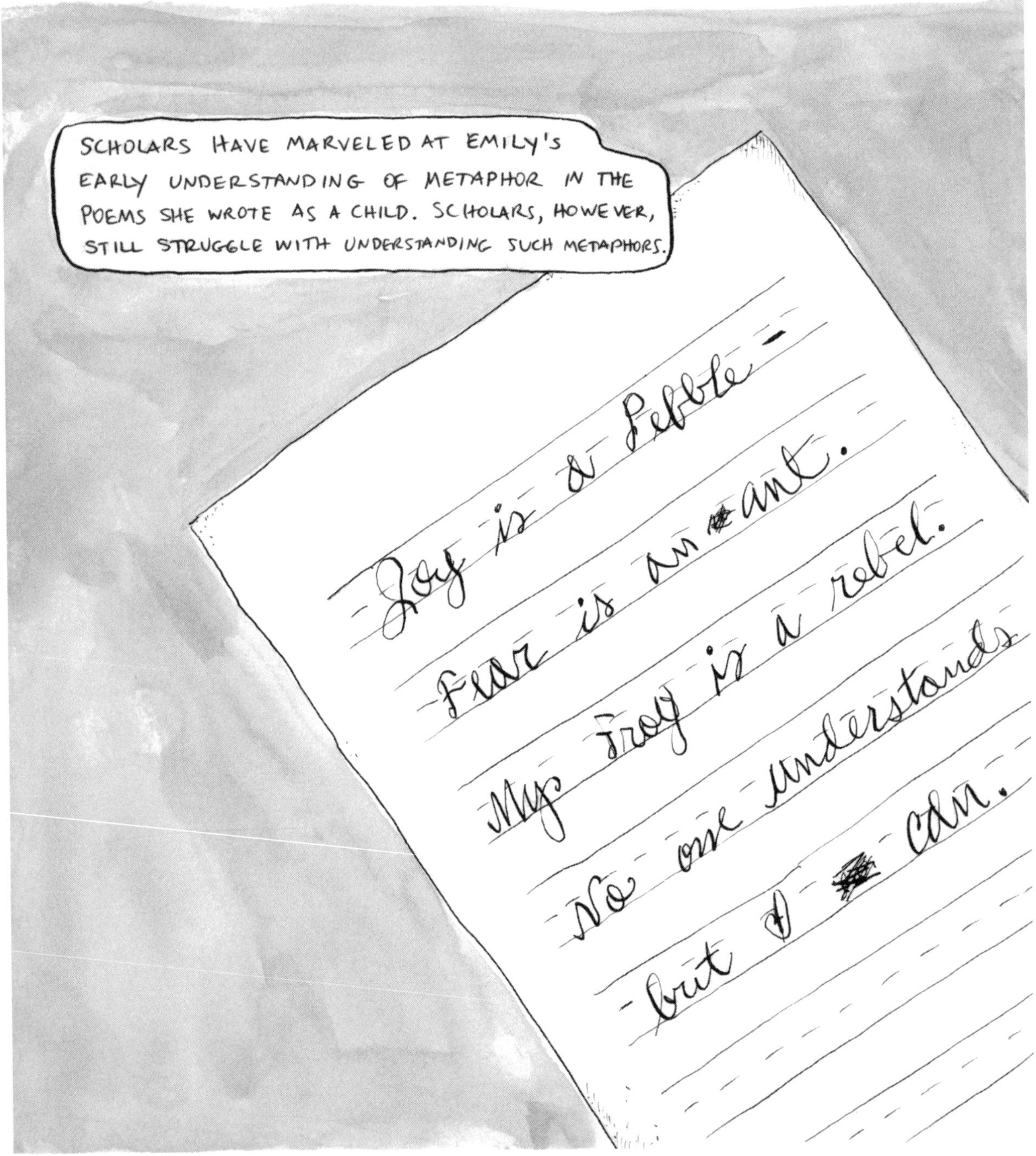

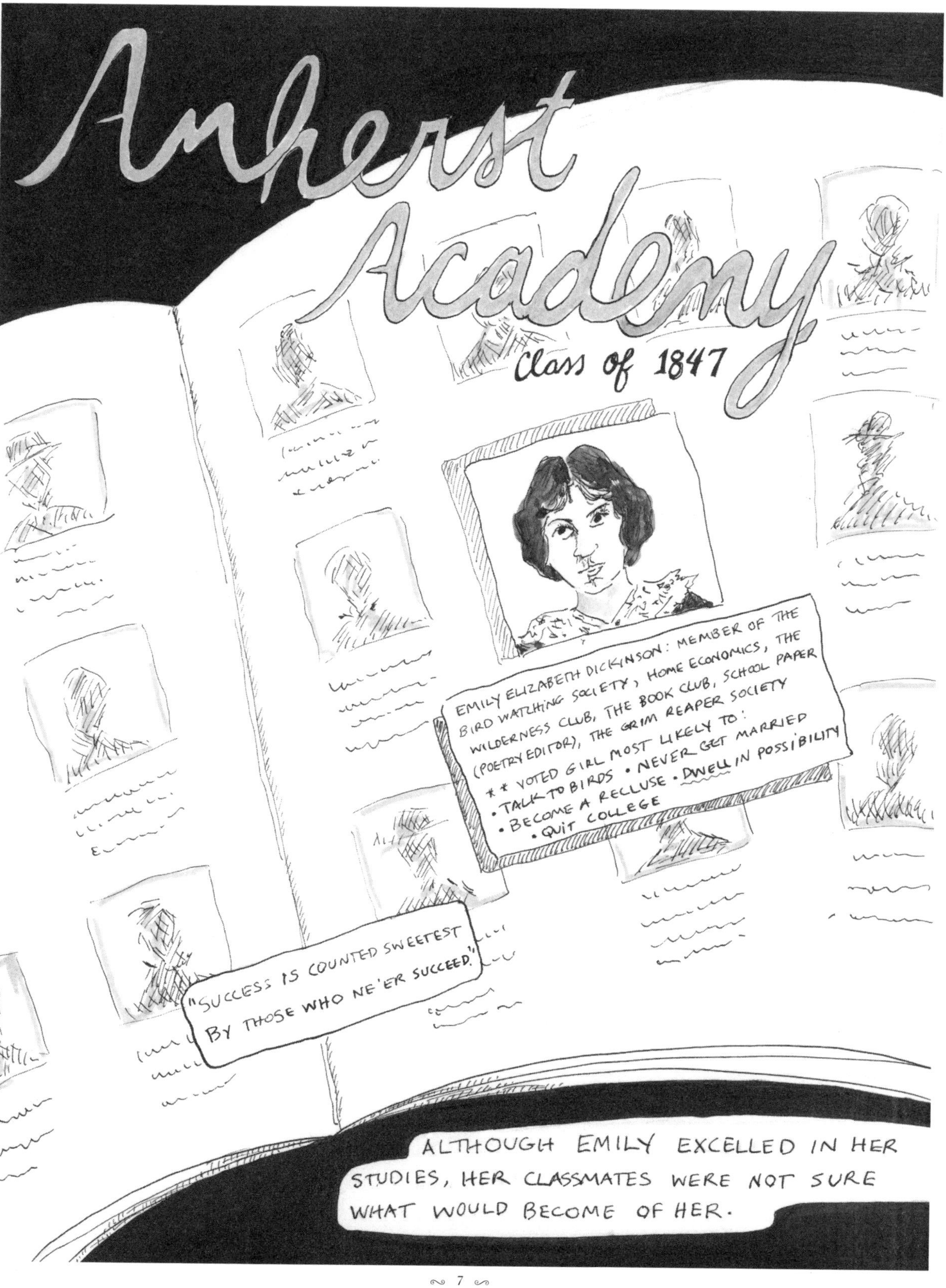
Amherst Academy
Class of 1847
EMILY ELIZABETH DICKINSON: MEMBER OF THE BIRD WATCHING SOCIETY, HOME ECONOMICS, THE WILDERNESS CLUB, THE BOOK CLUB, SCHOOL PAPER (POETRY EDITOR), THE GRIM REAPER SOCIETY
** VOTED GIRL MOST LIKELY TO:
• TALK TO BIRDS • NEVER GET MARRIED
• BECOME A RECLUSE • DWELL IN POSSIBILITY
• QUIT COLLEGE
"SUCCESS IS COUNTED SWEETEST BY THOSE WHO NE'ER SUCCEED."
ALTHOUGH EMILY EXCELLED IN HER STUDIES, HER CLASSMATES WERE NOT SURE WHAT WOULD BECOME OF HER.

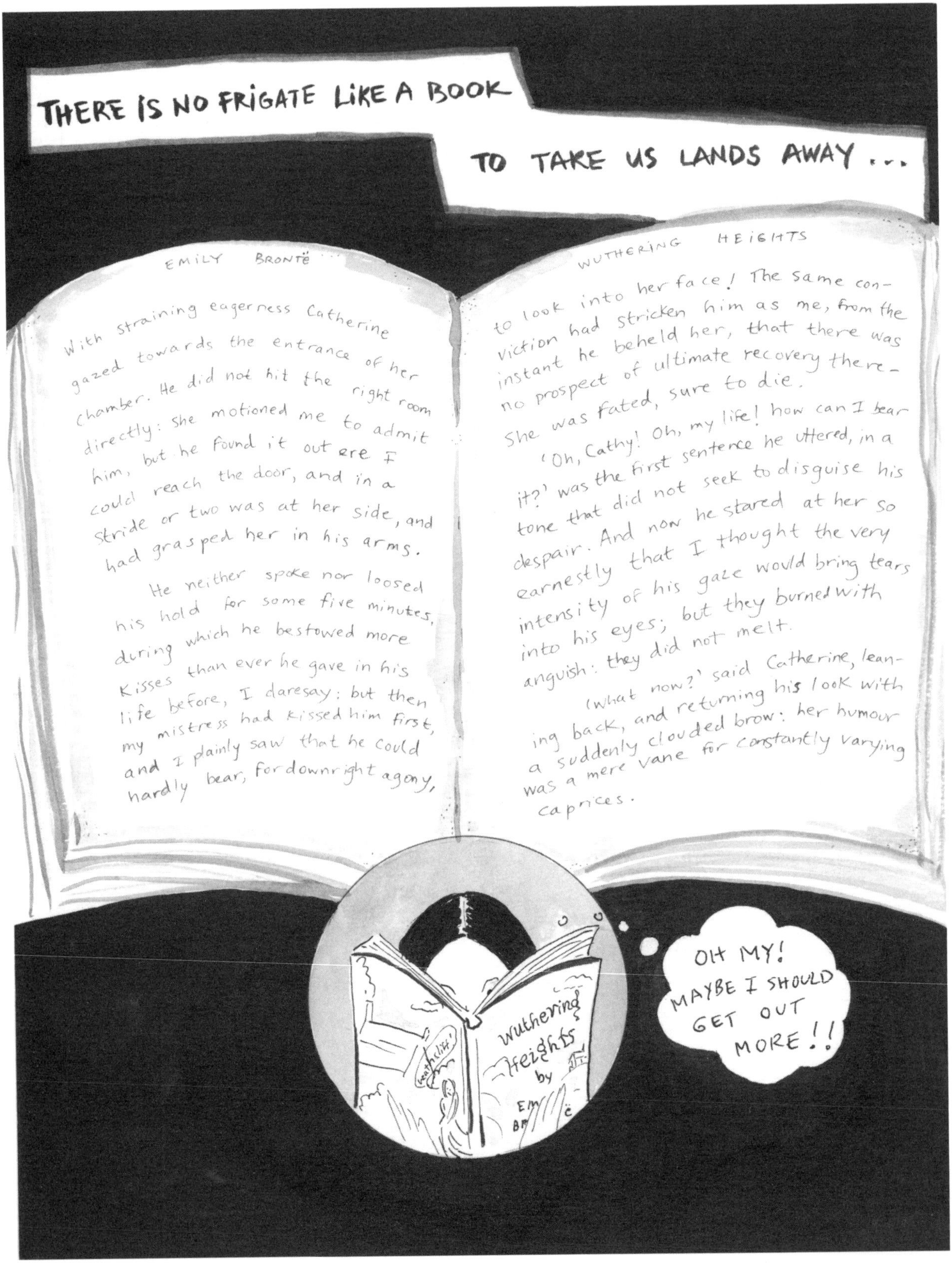
THERE IS NO FRIGATE LIKE A BOOK
TO TAKE US LANDS AWAY...
EMILY BRONTË
WUTHERING HEIGHTS
With straining eagerness Catherine gazed towards the entrance of her chamber. He did not hit the right room directly: she motioned me to admit him, but he found it out ere I could reach the door, and in a stride or two was at her side, and had grasped her in his arms.
He neither spoke nor loosed his hold for some five minutes, during which he bestowed more kisses than ever he gave in his life before, I daresay: but then my mistress had kissed him first, and I plainly saw that he could hardly bear, for downright agony,
to look into her face! The same conviction had stricken him as me, from the instant he beheld her, that there was no prospect of ultimate recovery there— She was fated, sure to die.
'Oh, Cathy! Oh, my life! how can I bear it?' was the first sentence he uttered, in a tone that did not seek to disguise his despair. And now he stared at her so earnestly that I thought the very intensity of his gaze would bring tears into his eyes; but they burned with anguish: they did not melt.
'What now?' said Catherine, leaning back, and returning his look with a suddenly clouded brow: her humour was a mere vane for constantly varying caprices.
Wuthering Heights by
OH MY! MAYBE I SHOULD GET OUT MORE!!

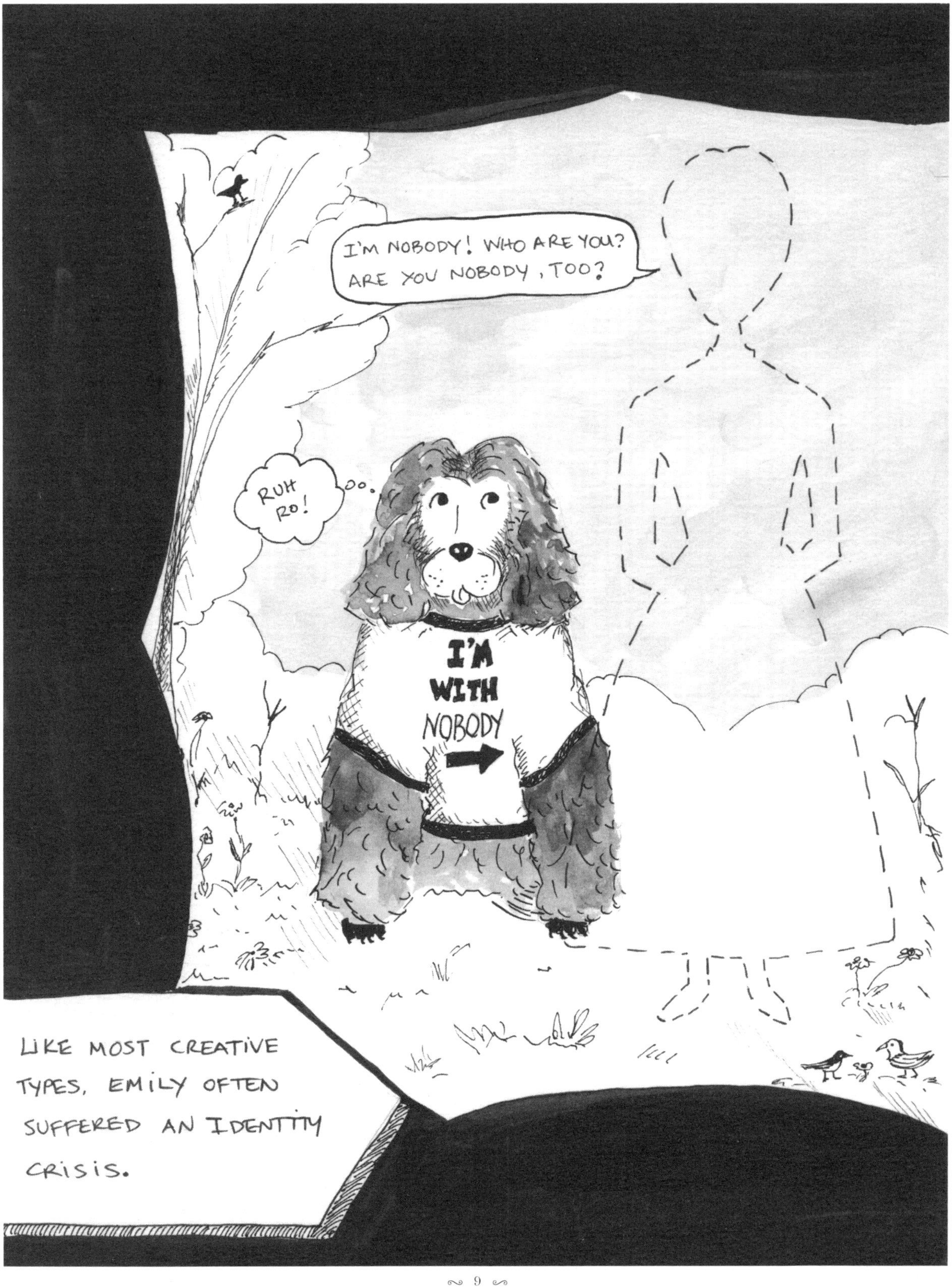
I'M NOBODY! WHO ARE YOU? ARE YOU NOBODY, TOO?
RUH RO!
I'M WITH NOBODY
LIKE MOST CREATIVE TYPES, EMILY OFTEN SUFFERED AN IDENTITY CRISIS.

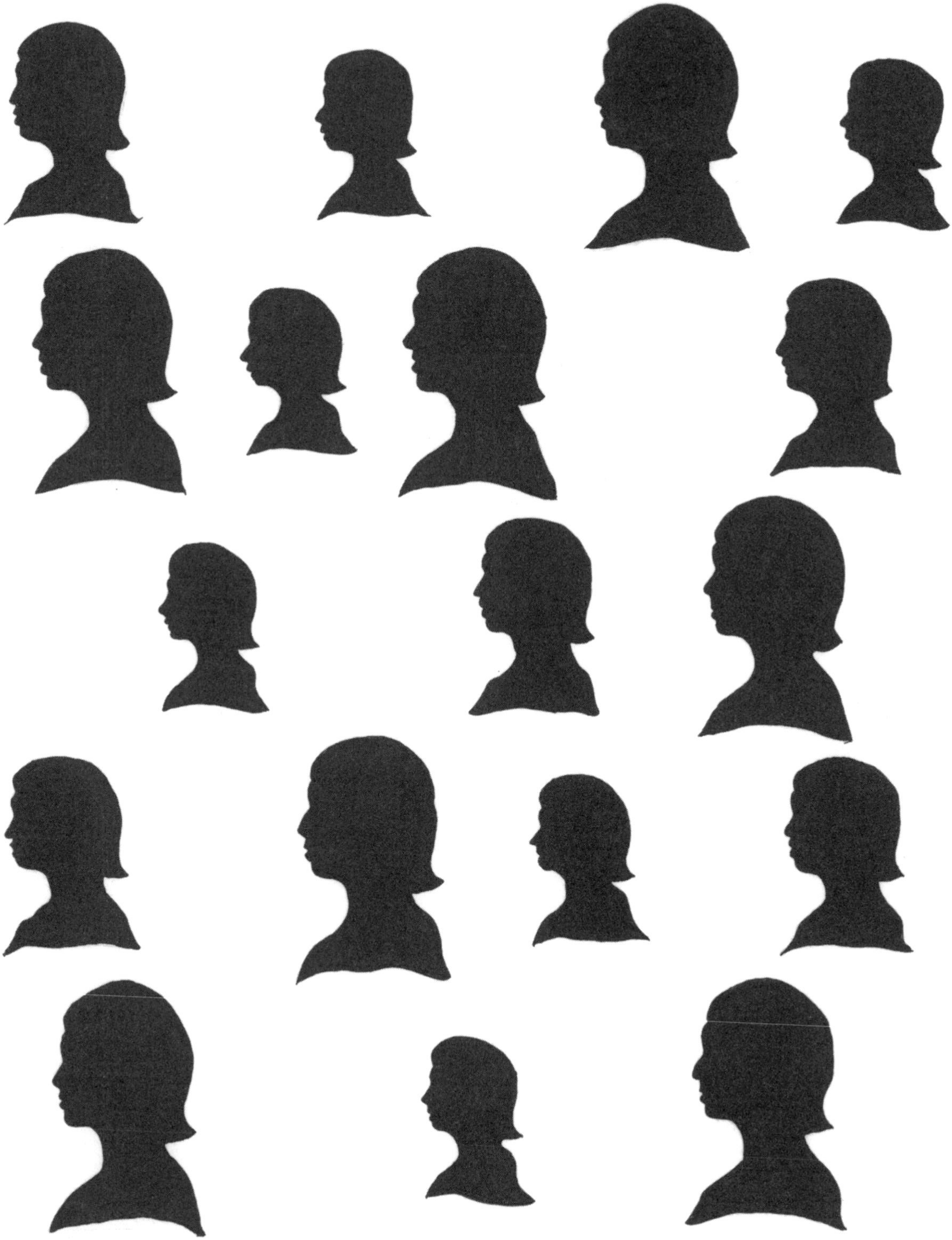

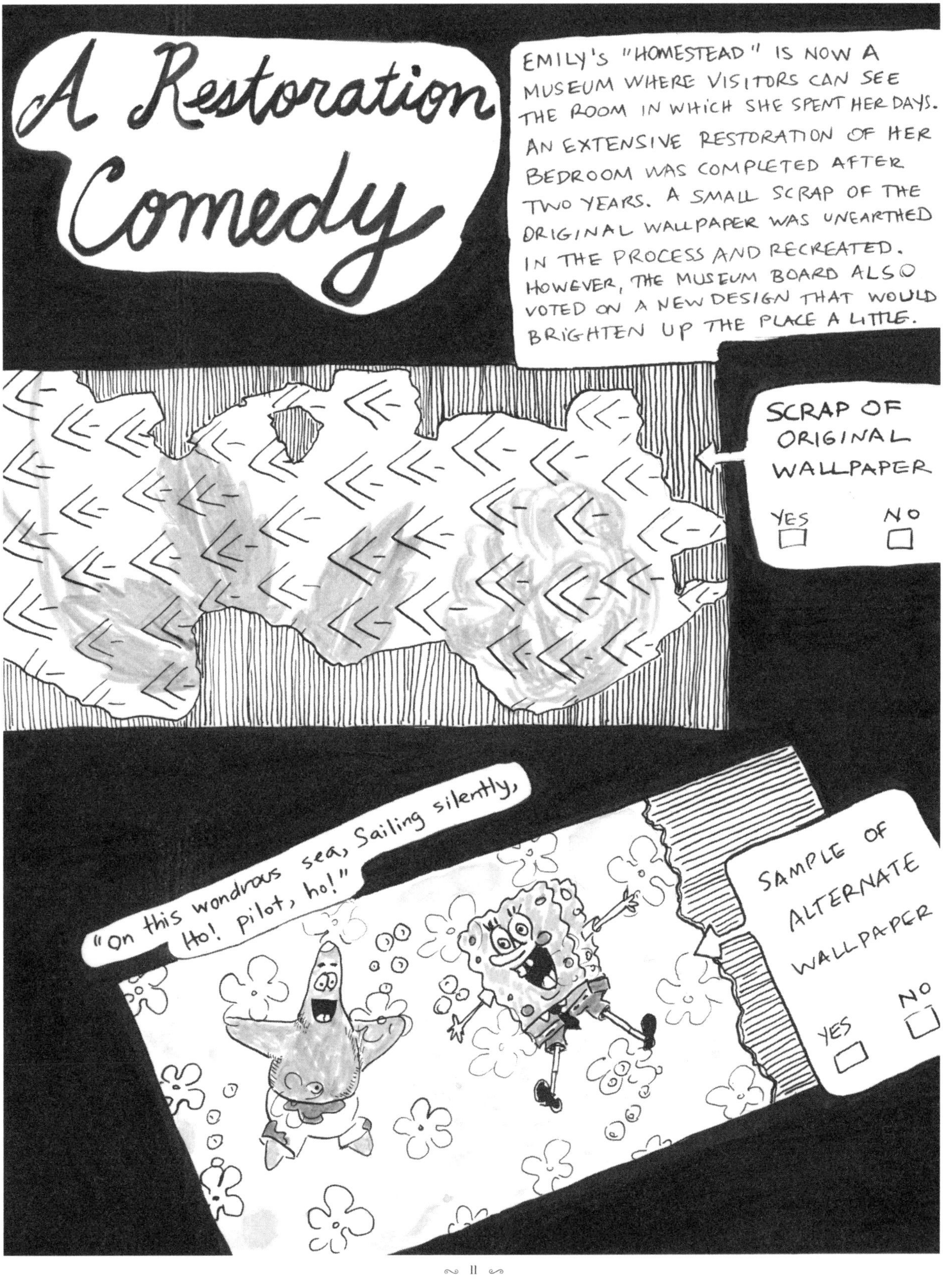
A Restoration Comedy
EMILY'S "HOMESTEAD" IS NOW A MUSEUM WHERE VISITORS CAN SEE THE ROOM IN WHICH SHE SPENT HER DAYS. AN EXTENSIVE RESTORATION OF HER BEDROOM WAS COMPLETED AFTER TWO YEARS. A SMALL SCRAP OF THE ORIGINAL WALLPAPER WAS UNEARTHED IN THE PROCESS AND RECREATED. HOWEVER, THE MUSEUM BOARD ALSO VOTED ON A NEW DESIGN THAT WOULD BRIGHTEN UP THE PLACE A LITTLE.
SCRAP OF ORIGINAL WALLPAPER
YES
NO
"On this wondrous sea, Sailing silently, Ho! pilot, ho!"
SAMPLE OF ALTERNATE WALLPAPER
YES
NO

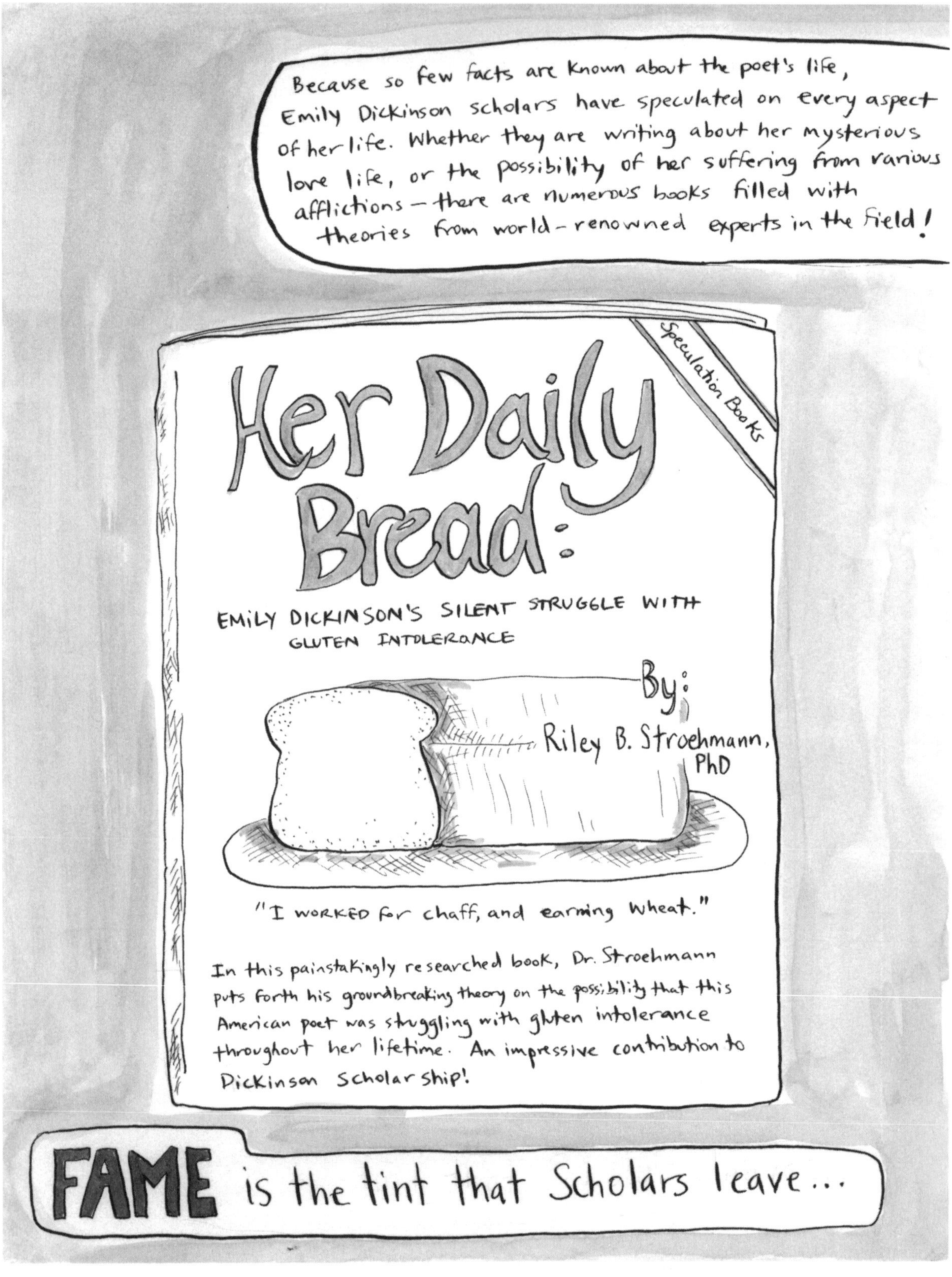
Because so few facts are known about the poet's life, Emily Dickinson scholars have speculated on every aspect of her life. Whether they are writing about her mysterious love life, or the possibility of her suffering from various afflictions — there are numerous books filled with theories from world-renowned experts in the field!
Speculation Books
Her Daily Bread:
EMILY DICKINSON'S SILENT STRUGGLE WITH GLUTEN INTOLERANCE
By: Riley B. Stroehmann, PhD
"I WORKED for chaff, and earning Wheat."
In this painstakingly researched book, Dr. Stroehmann puts forth his groundbreaking theory on the possibility that this American poet was struggling with gluten intolerance throughout her lifetime. An impressive contribution to Dickinson Scholarship!
FAME is the tint that Scholars leave...

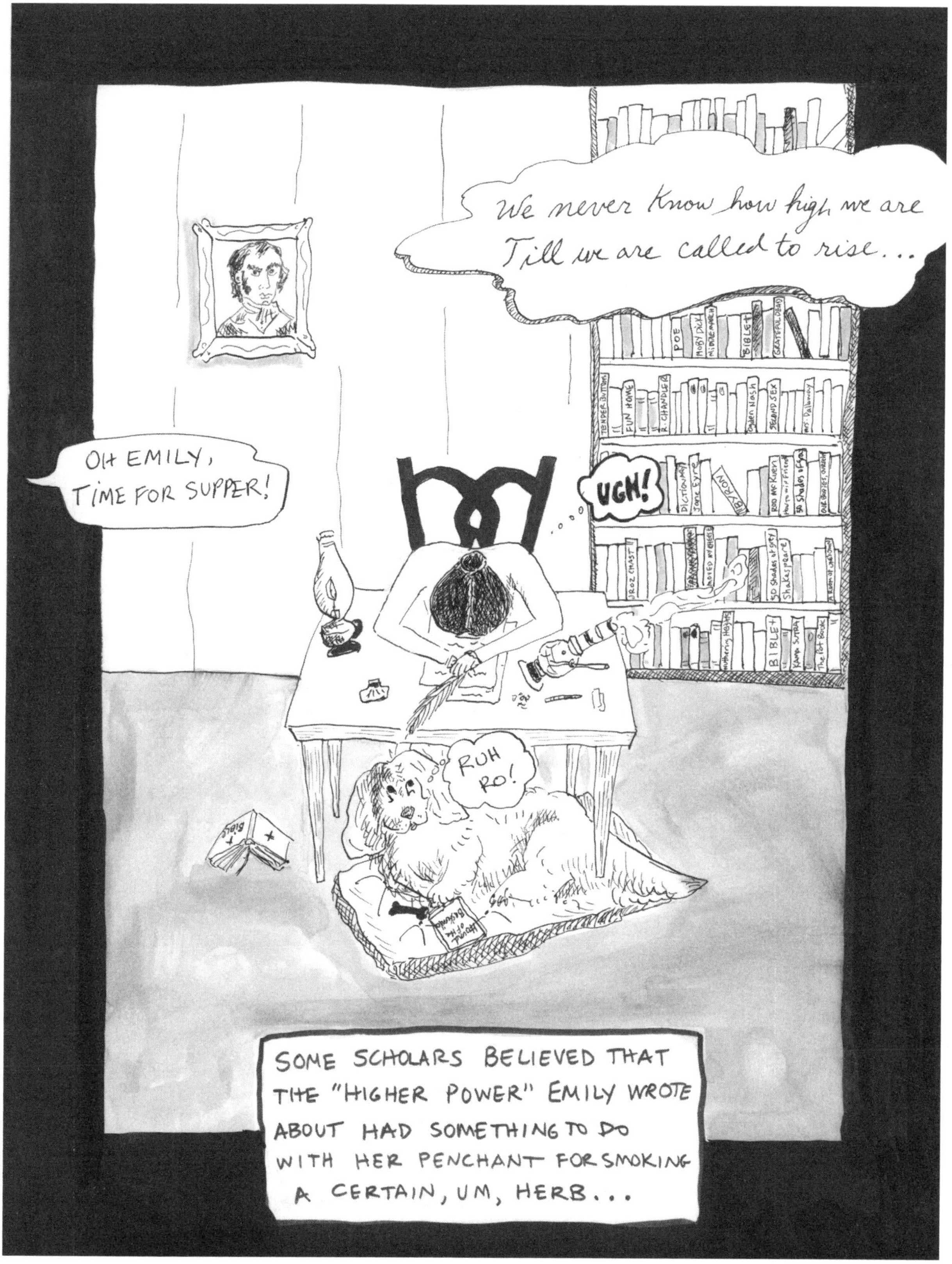
We never know how high we are
Till we are called to rise...
OH EMILY, TIME FOR SUPPER!
UGH!
RUH RO!
SOME SCHOLARS BELIEVED THAT THE "HIGHER POWER" EMILY WROTE ABOUT HAD SOMETHING TO DO WITH HER PENCHANT FOR SMOKING A CERTAIN, UM, HERB...

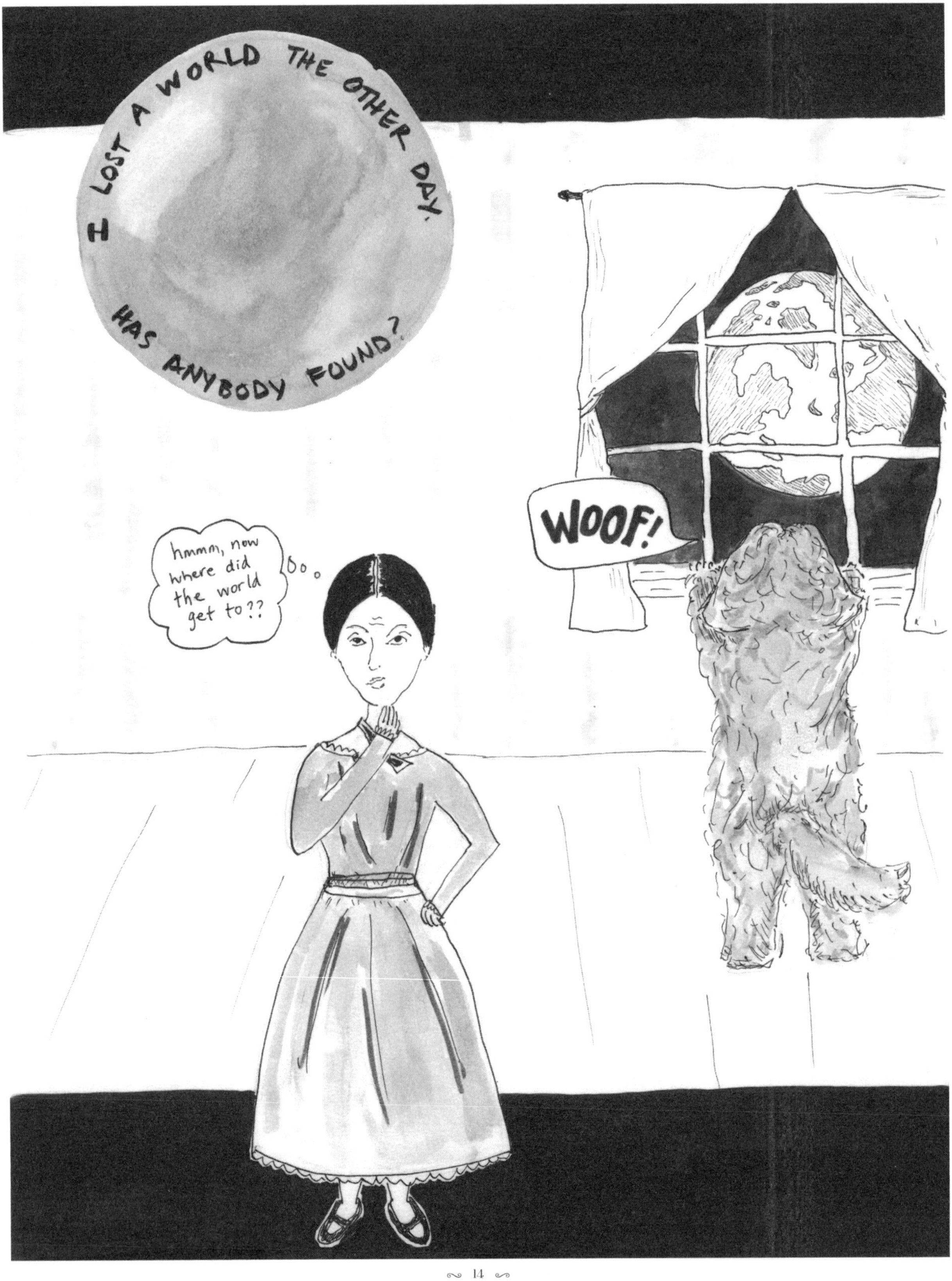
I LOST A WORLD THE OTHER DAY.
HAS ANYBODY FOUND?
WOOF!
hmmm, now where did the world get to??

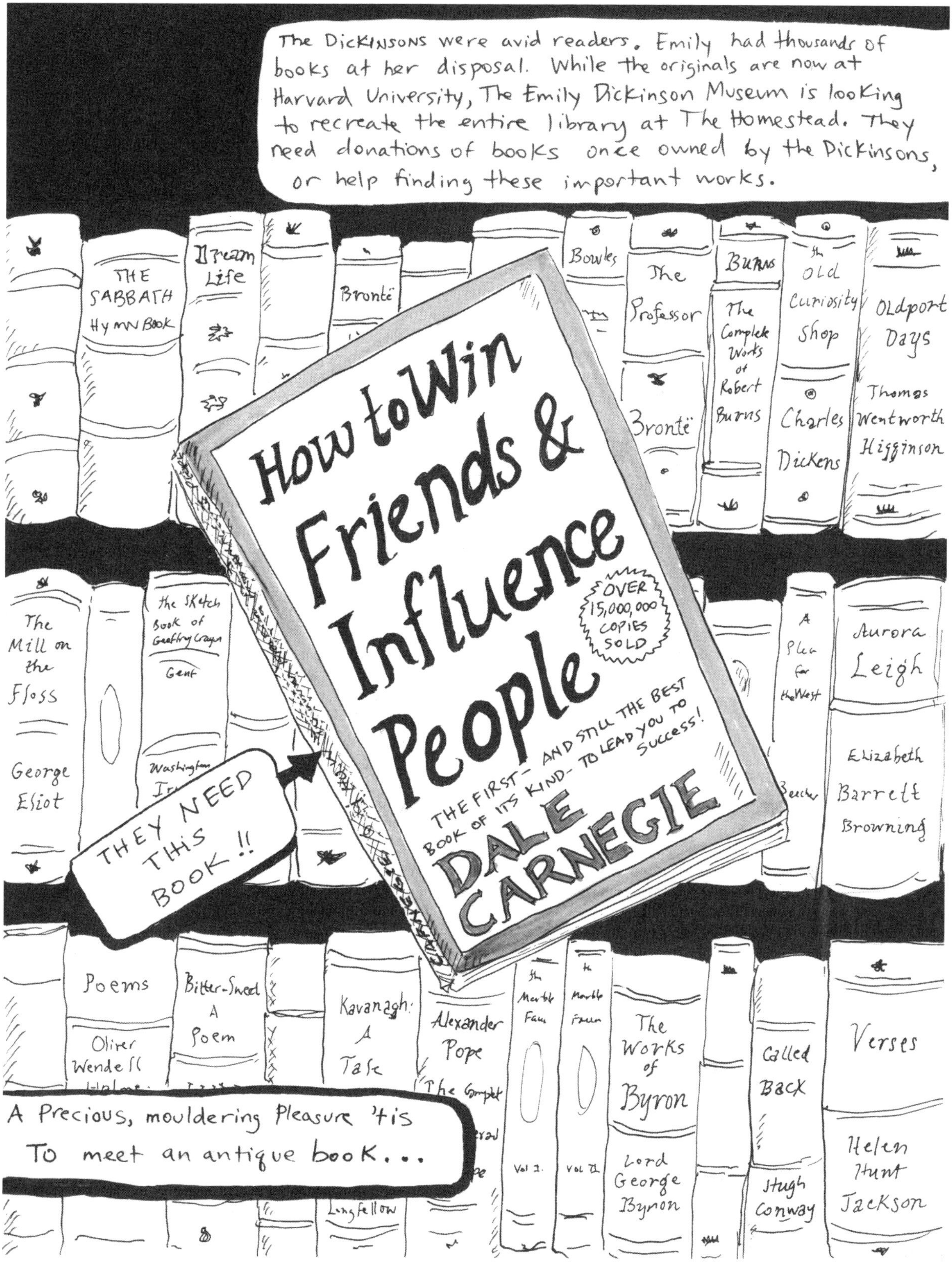

The Dickinsons were avid readers. Emily had thousands of books at her disposal. While the originals are now at Harvard University, The Emily Dickinson Museum is looking to recreate the entire library at The Homestead. They need donations of books once owned by the Dickinsons, or help finding these important works.
THE SABBATH HYMN BOOK
Dream Life
Brontë
Bowles
The Professor Brontë
Burns The Complete Works of Robert Burns
The Old Curiosity Shop Charles Dickens
Oldport Days Thomas Wentworth Higginson
How to Win Friends & Influence People
OVER 15,000,000 COPIES SOLD
THE FIRST—AND STILL THE BEST BOOK OF ITS KIND—TO LEAD YOU TO SUCCESS!
DALE CARNEGIE
The Mill on the Floss George Eliot
the Sketch Book of Geoffrey Crayon Gent
A Plea for the West
Beecher
Aurora Leigh Elizabeth Barrett Browning
THEY NEED THIS BOOK!!
Poems Oliver Wendell
Bitter-Sweet A Poem
Kavanagh: A Tale
Longfellow
Alexander Pope
The Marble Faun Vol I.
The Marble Faun Vol II
The Works of Byron Lord George Byron
Called Back Hugh Conway
Verses Helen Hunt Jackson
A Precious, mouldering Pleasure 'tis To meet an antique book...

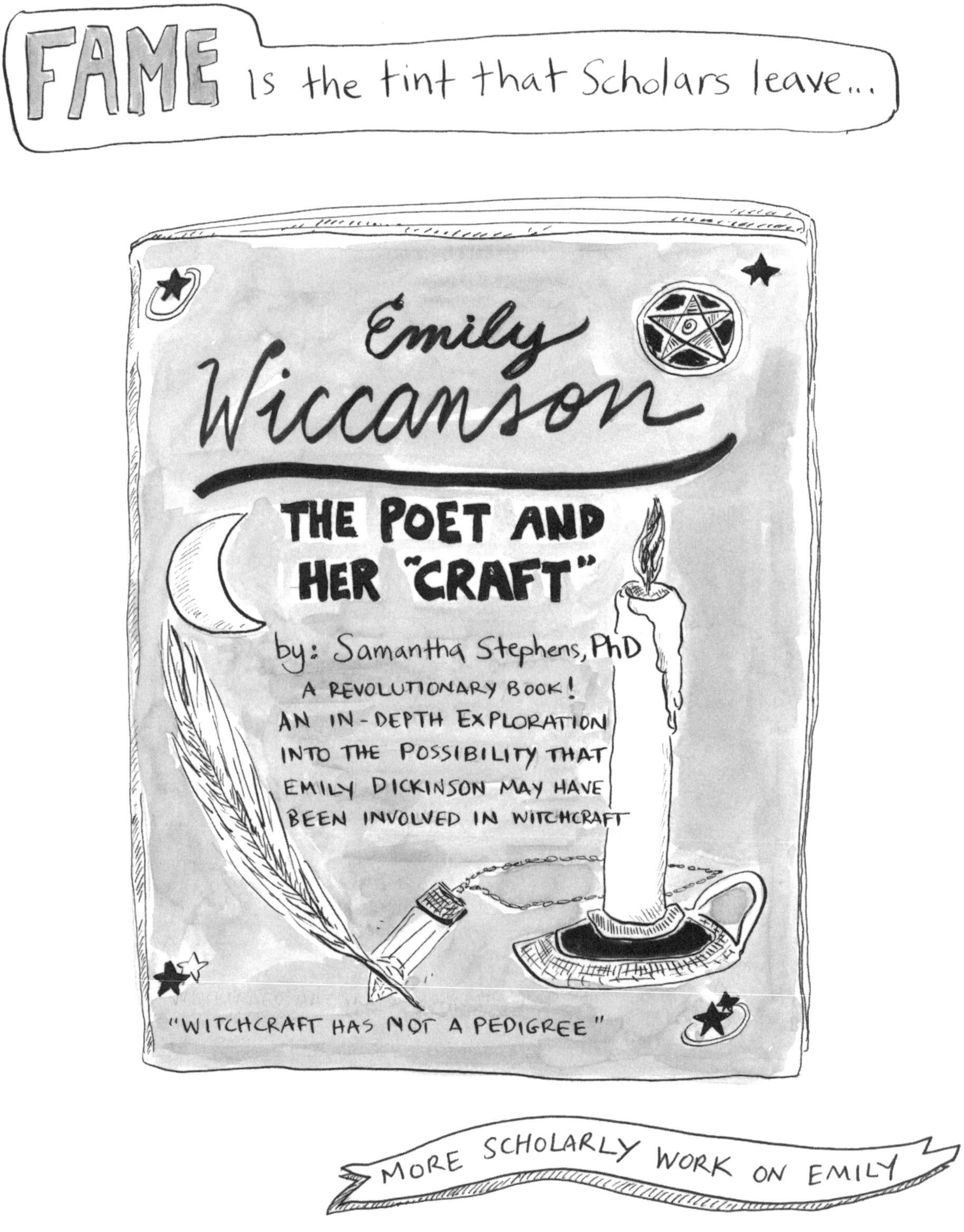
FAME is the tint that Scholars leave...
Emily Wiccanson
THE POET AND HER "CRAFT"
by: Samantha Stephens, PhD
A REVOLUTIONARY BOOK!
AN IN-DEPTH EXPLORATION INTO THE POSSIBILITY THAT EMILY DICKINSON MAY HAVE BEEN INVOLVED IN WITCHCRAFT
"WITCHCRAFT HAS NOT A PEDIGREE"
MORE SCHOLARLY WORK ON EMILY

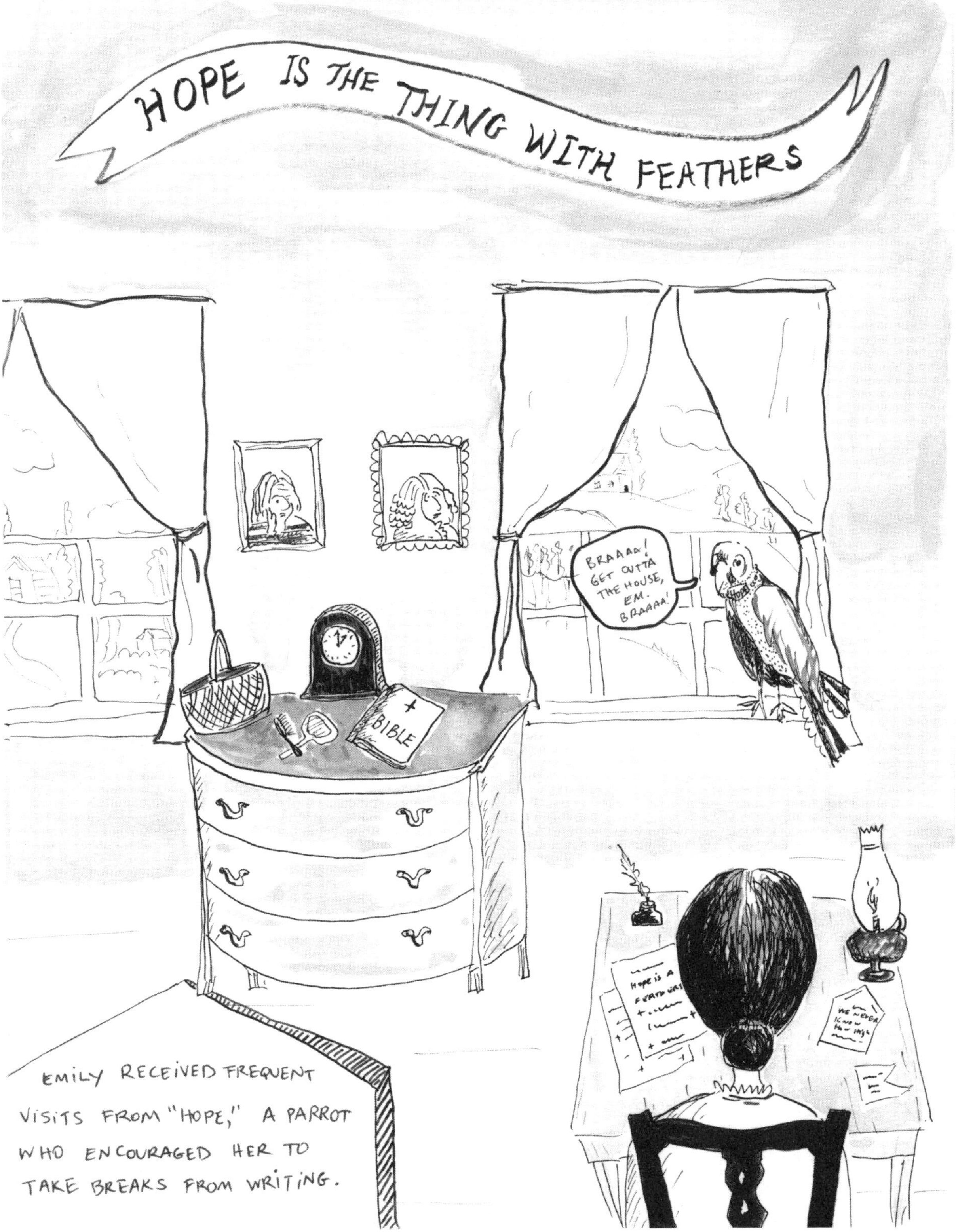
HOPE IS THE THING WITH FEATHERS
BRAAAA! GET OUTTA THE HOUSE, EM. BRAAAA!
BIBLE
EMILY RECEIVED FREQUENT VISITS FROM "HOPE," A PARROT WHO ENCOURAGED HER TO TAKE BREAKS FROM WRITING.

MORE FROM THE EMILY DICKINSON LIBRARY PROJECT
Fun Home Alison Bechdel
Are you my mother? Alison Bechdel
Hark! A Vagrant Kate Beaton
Truth is Fragmentary
Cruddy Lynda Barry
ONE! Hundred! Demons! Lynda Barry
Can't we Talk About Something more pleasant? Roz Chast
The Freddie Stories Lynda Barry
Easy Mimi Pond
The Secret Rhonda Byrne
The Party, after you left Roz Chast
The Voyeurs Gabrielle Bell
THEY NEED THIS BOOK!!
What I Hate: From A to Z Roz Chast
Fun Home Alison Bechdel
Dykes to watch out For Alison Bechdel
And the Pursuit of Happiness Maira Kalman
Persepolis Marjane Satrapi
Collected works of Ramona Fradon
Bossypants Tina Fey

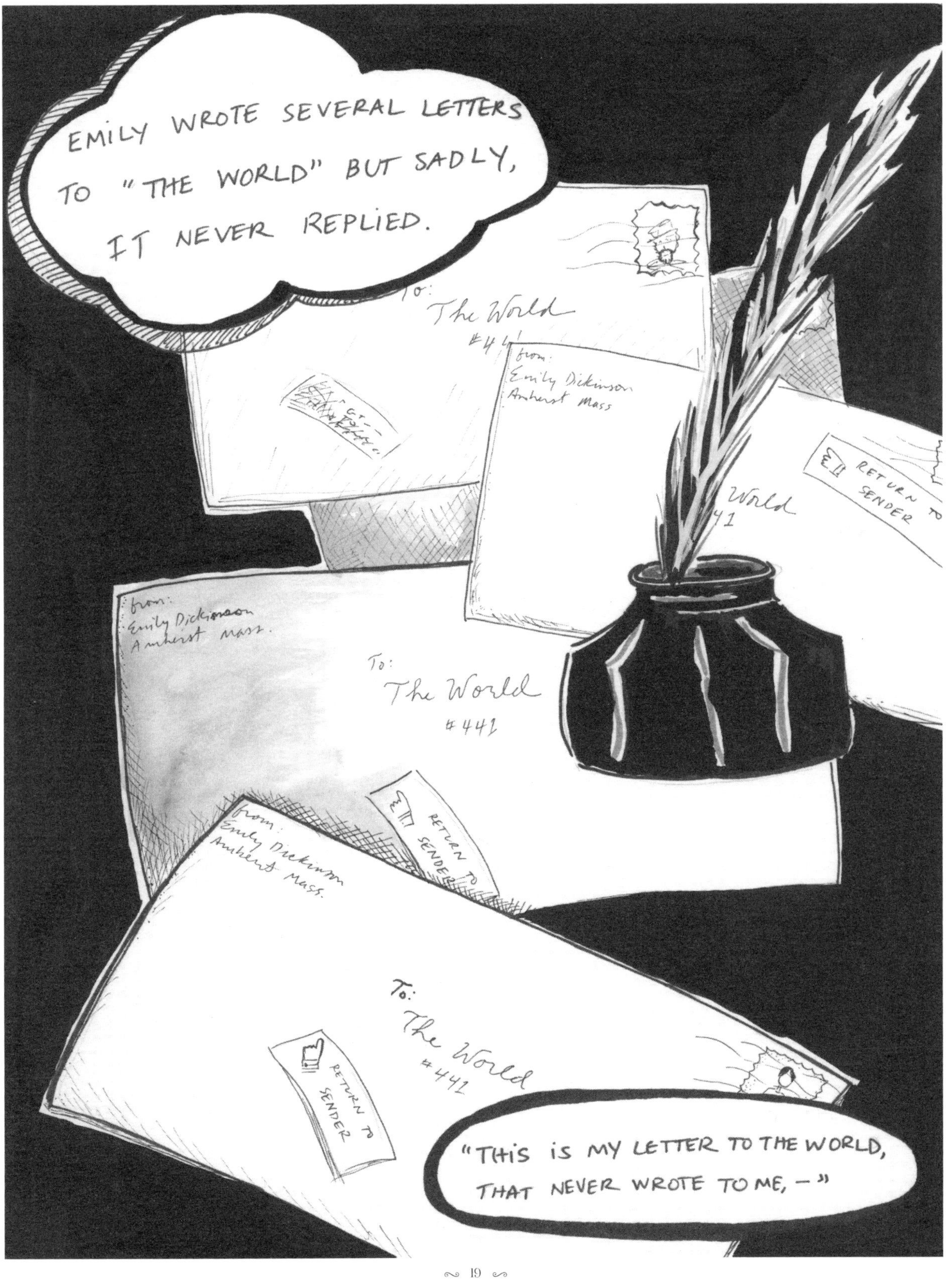
EMILY WROTE SEVERAL LETTERS TO "THE WORLD" BUT SADLY, IT NEVER REPLIED.
To: The World
from: Emily Dickinson Amherst Mass
RETURN TO SENDER
from: Emily Dickinson Amherst Mass.
To: The World #441
RETURN TO SENDER
from: Emily Dickinson Amherst Mass.
To: The World #442
RETURN TO SENDER
"THIS IS MY LETTER TO THE WORLD, THAT NEVER WROTE TO ME, –"

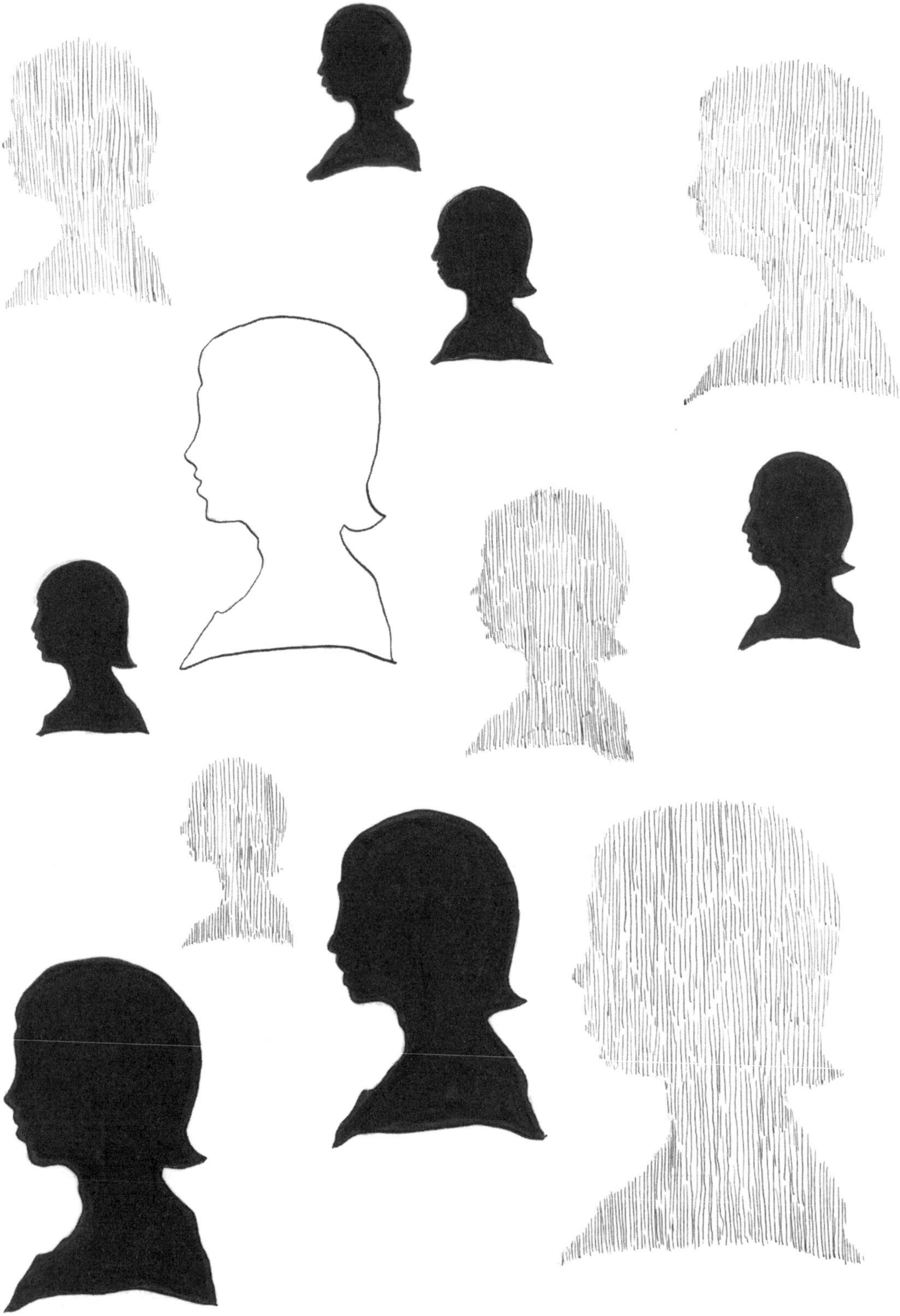

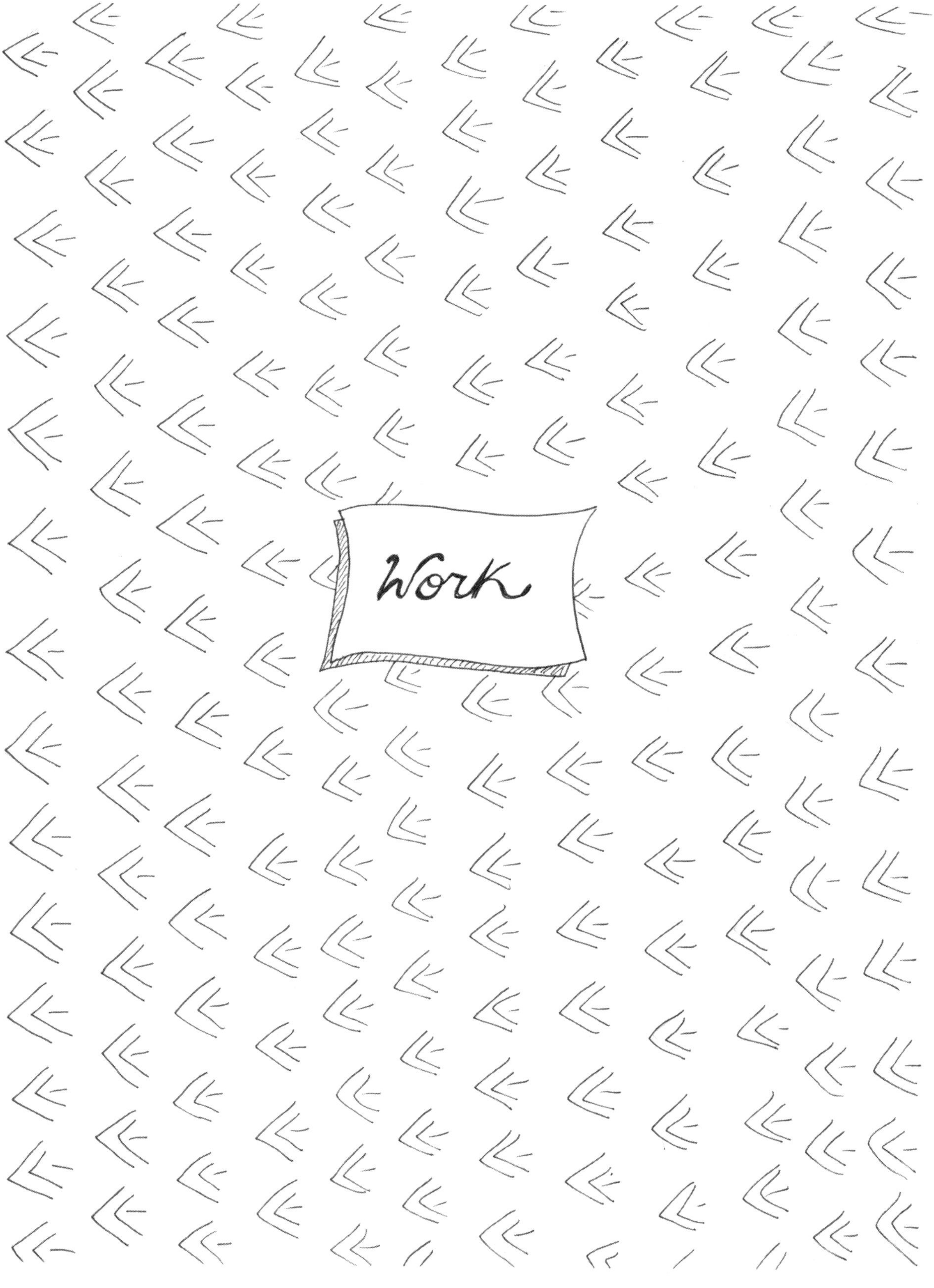
Work

EMILY DEFINES POETRY
If I feel physically as if the top of my head were taken off, I know that is POETRY.
POET BOBBLE HEAD DOLL
POET

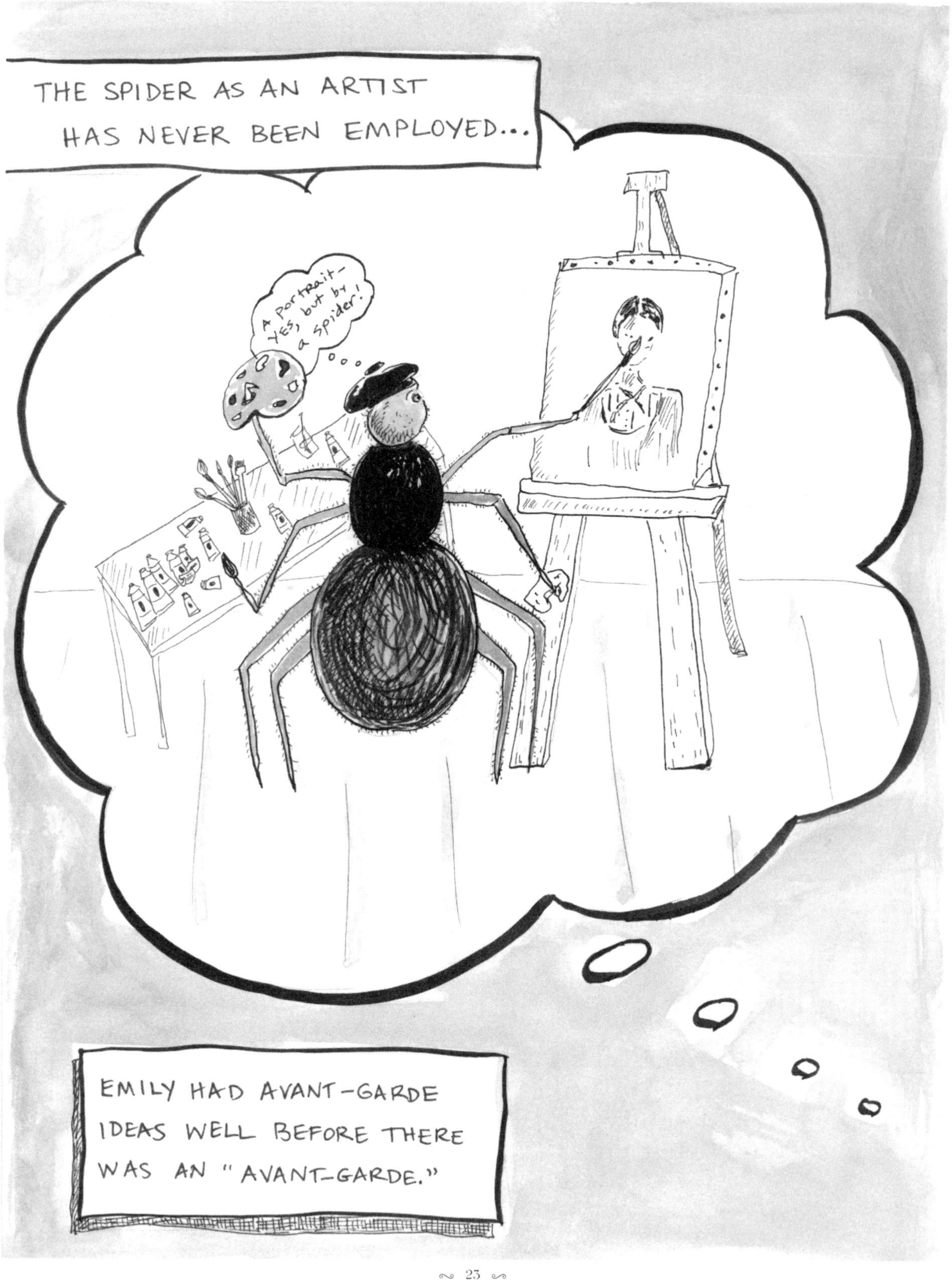
THE SPIDER AS AN ARTIST HAS NEVER BEEN EMPLOYED...
A portrait- YES, but by a spider!
EMILY HAD AVANT-GARDE IDEAS WELL BEFORE THERE WAS AN "AVANT-GARDE."

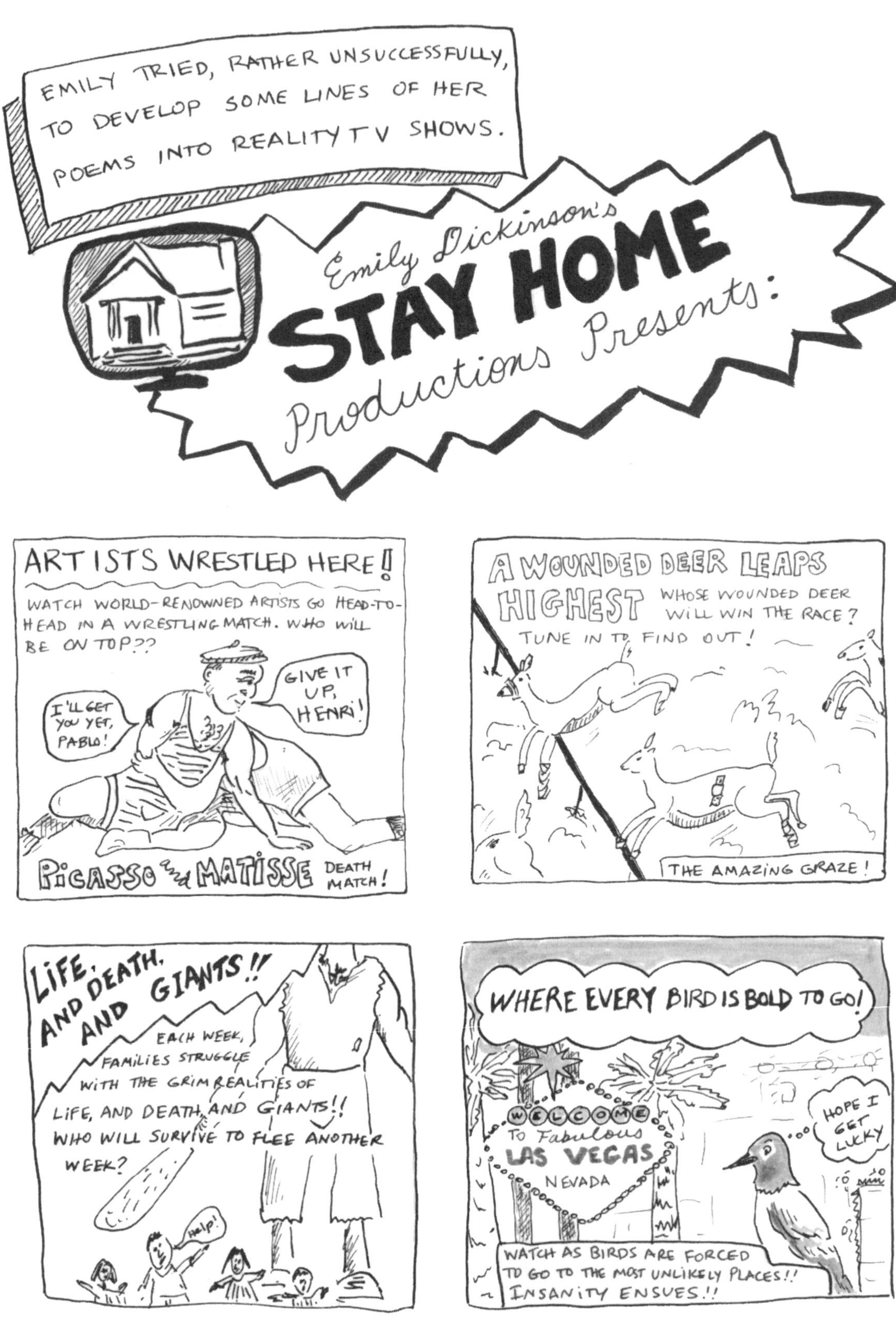

EMILY TRIED, RATHER UNSUCCESSFULLY, TO DEVELOP SOME LINES OF HER POEMS INTO REALITY TV SHOWS.
Emily Dickinson's
STAY HOME
Productions Presents:
ARTISTS WRESTLED HERE!
WATCH WORLD-RENOWNED ARTISTS GO HEAD-TO-HEAD IN A WRESTLING MATCH. WHO WILL BE ON TOP??
I'LL GET YOU YET, PABLO!
GIVE IT UP, HENRI!
PICASSO and MATISSE DEATH MATCH!
A WOUNDED DEER LEAPS HIGHEST
WHOSE WOUNDED DEER WILL WIN THE RACE? TUNE IN TO FIND OUT!
THE AMAZING GRAZE!
LIFE, AND DEATH, AND GIANTS!!
EACH WEEK, FAMILIES STRUGGLE WITH THE GRIM REALITIES OF LIFE, AND DEATH, AND GIANTS!! WHO WILL SURVIVE TO FLEE ANOTHER WEEK?
Help!
WHERE EVERY BIRD IS BOLD TO GO!
WELCOME To Fabulous LAS VEGAS NEVADA
HOPE I GET LUCKY
WATCH AS BIRDS ARE FORCED TO GO TO THE MOST UNLIKELY PLACES!! INSANITY ENSUES!!

A WOMAN OF Letters

EMILY'S OUTPUT INCLUDES THOUSANDS OF LETTERS. OFTEN, SHE ENCLOSED SPECIAL GIFTS FOR HER LOVED ONES — SUCH AS:

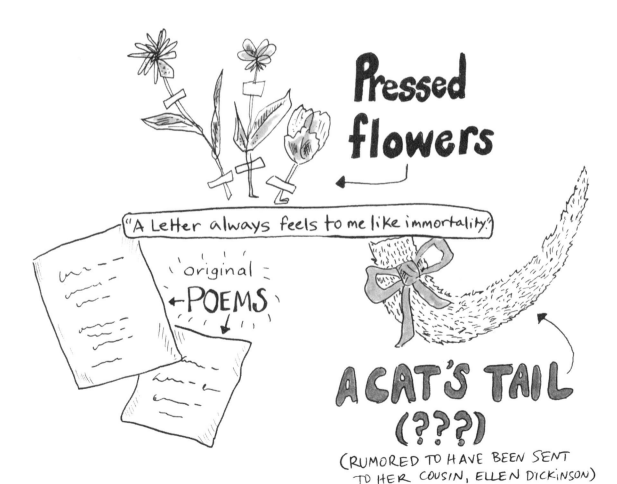

Pressed flowers

"A letter always feels to me like immortality."

'original' → POEMS

A CAT'S TAIL (???)

(RUMORED TO HAVE BEEN SENT TO HER COUSIN, ELLEN DICKINSON)

The AMHERST

Ask Emily!

Dear Emily,

I am out of sorts, as my husband of 20 years has been spending a considerable amount of time away from our home. God only knows what he is up to! Whenever I ask him where he has been, he insists that he has important business to attend to and that it doesn't concern me. I fear he may be seeing another woman. I lose sleep each night just thinking about it. What shall I do? How might I save my marriage? Signed, **WIFE IN STRIFE**

Dear **WIFE IN STRIFE,**

There is another Loneliness
That many die without,
Not want or friend occasions it,
Or circumstances or lot.

GAZETTE

Dear Emily,

My best friend has been acting strangely of late. We used to get together and talk of our woes and sometimes we would get drunk as forty billy goats. Lately, however, he puts me off and claims there is too much work to do on his farm. Are his cattle more important than his best friend and long time drinking pal? Signed, **LONELY IN SPIRITS**

Dear **LONELY IN SPIRITS,**

Are friends delight or pain?
Could bounty but remain
   Riches were good.

AMONG THE MANY INDUSTRIOUS ACTIVITIES EMILY TRIED IN ORDER TO SUPPORT HER ART WAS A SHORT-LIVED STINT AS AN ADVICE COLUMNIST.

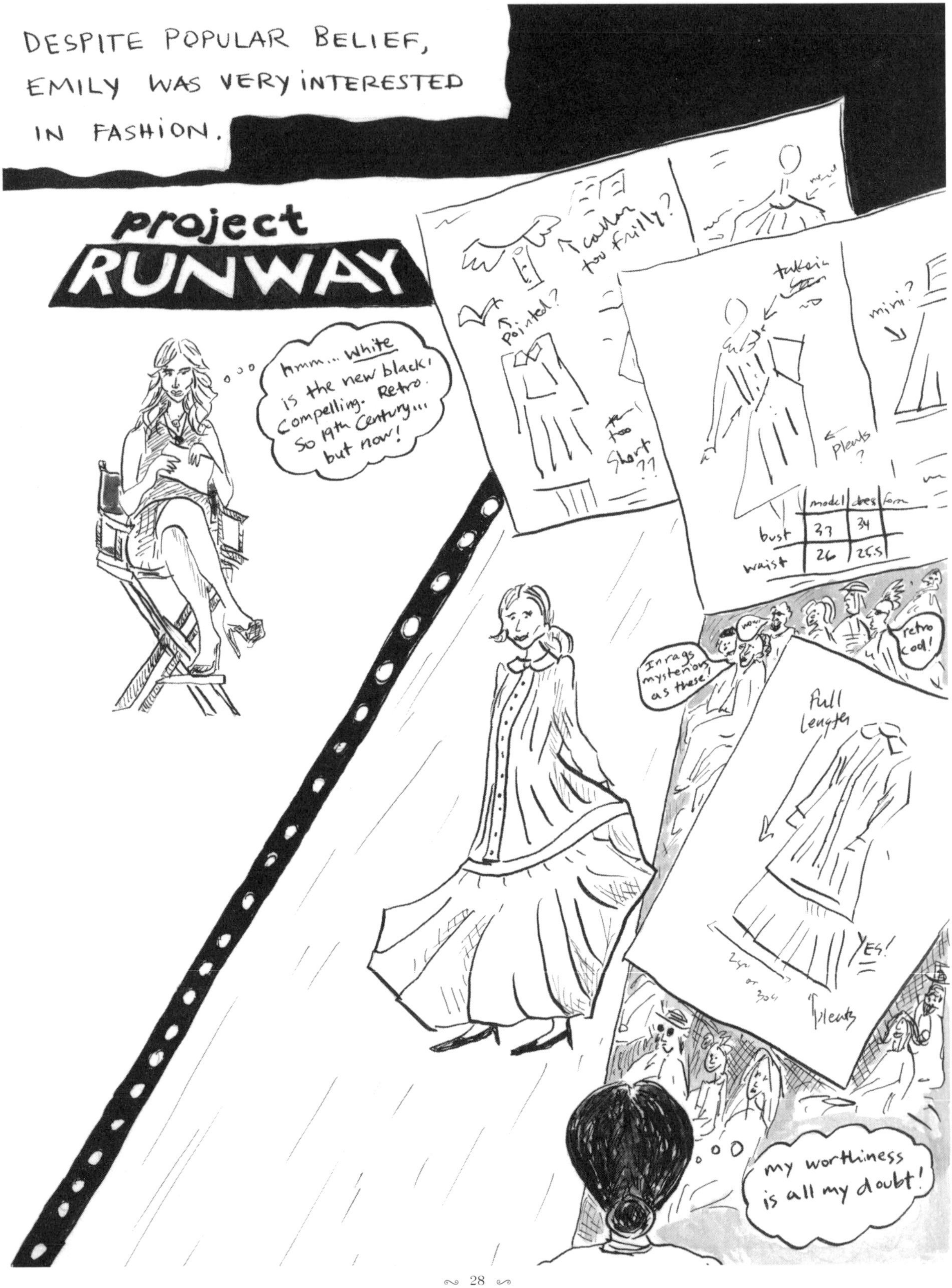
DESPITE POPULAR BELIEF, EMILY WAS VERY INTERESTED IN FASHION.
project RUNWAY
hmm... White is the new black! Compelling. Retro. So 19th Century... but now!
collar too frilly?
pointed?
too Short ??
take in
mini?
pleats ?
model dress form
bust 33 34
waist 26 25.5
In rags mysterious as these!
wow
retro cool!
Full Length
YES!
pleats
my worthiness is all my doubt!

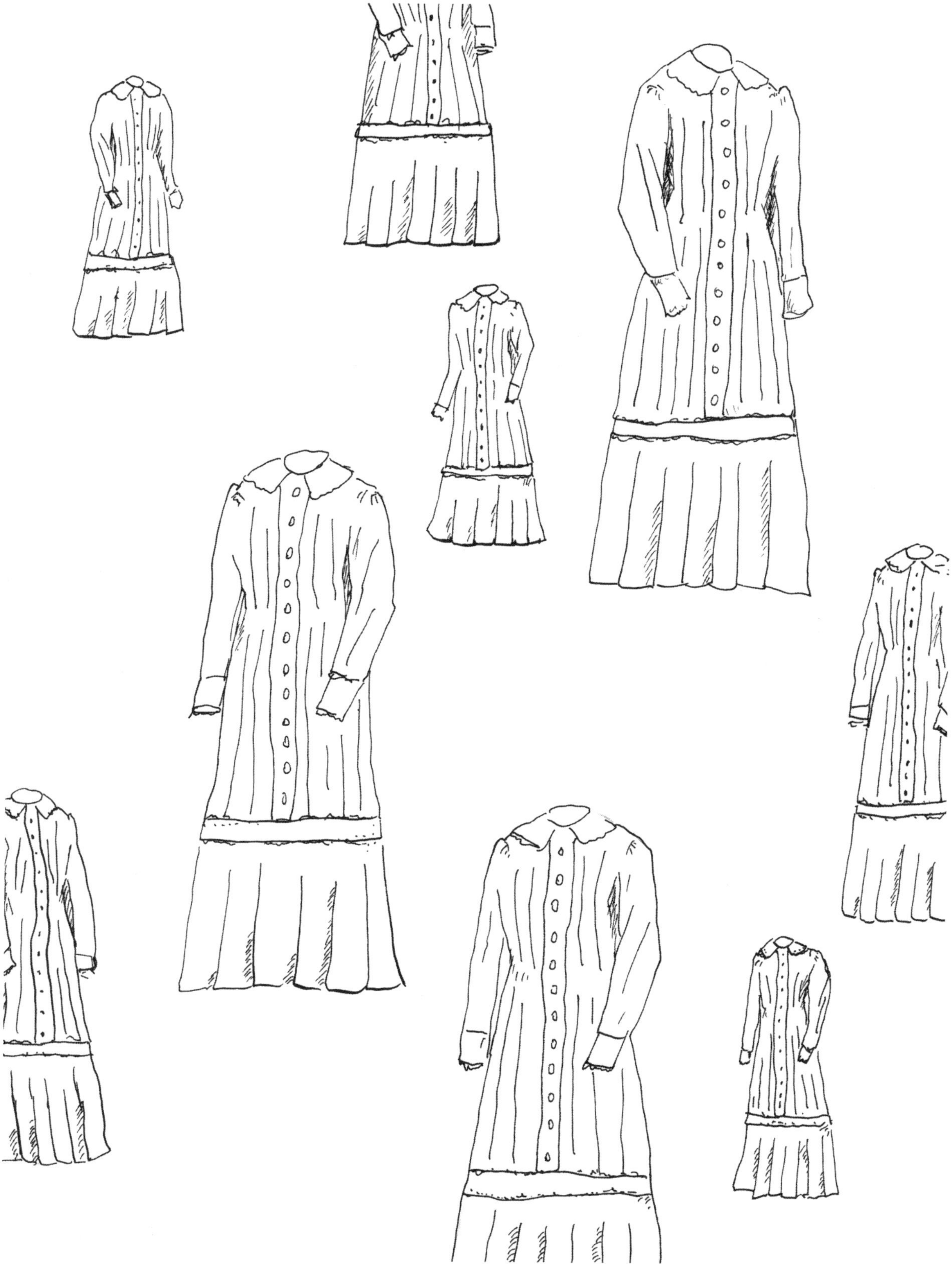

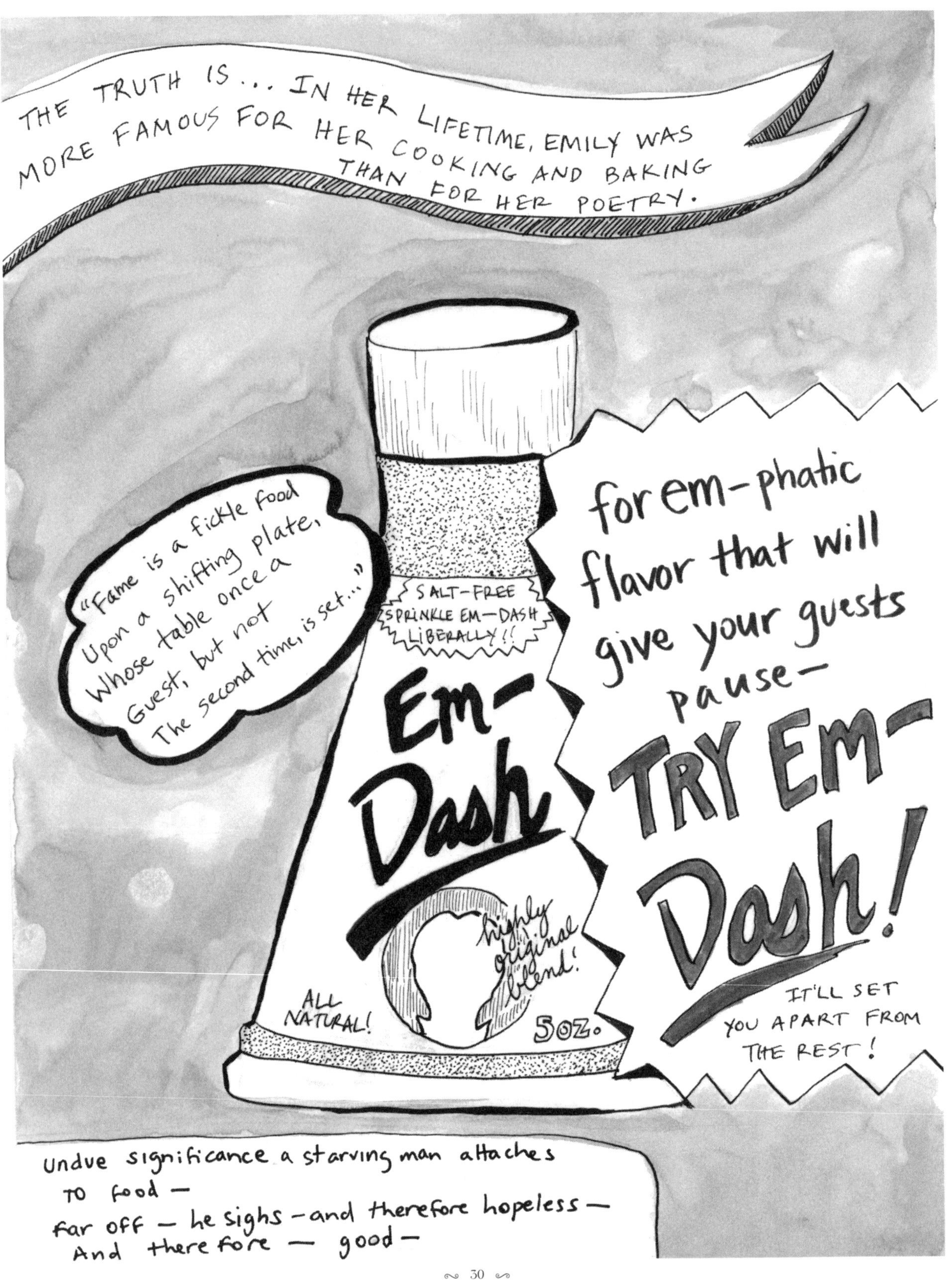

THE TRUTH IS... IN HER LIFETIME, EMILY WAS MORE FAMOUS FOR HER COOKING AND BAKING THAN FOR HER POETRY.
"Fame is a fickle food Upon a shifting plate, Whose table once a Guest, but not The second time, is set..."
SALT-FREE SPRINKLE EM-DASH LIBERALLY!!
Em-Dash
highly original blend!
ALL NATURAL!
5OZ.
for em-phatic flavor that will give your guests pause-
TRY EM-Dash!
IT'LL SET YOU APART FROM THE REST!
Undue significance a starving man attaches to food—
Far off — he sighs—and therefore hopeless—
And therefore — good—

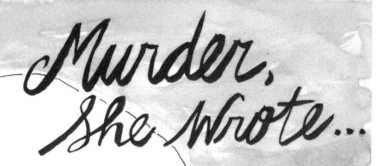

Murder, She Wrote...

She died, – this was the way she died; And when her breath was done, Took up her simple wardrobe And started for the sun.

During periods of self-doubt about being a poet, EMILY sometimes dabbled in writing detective stories.

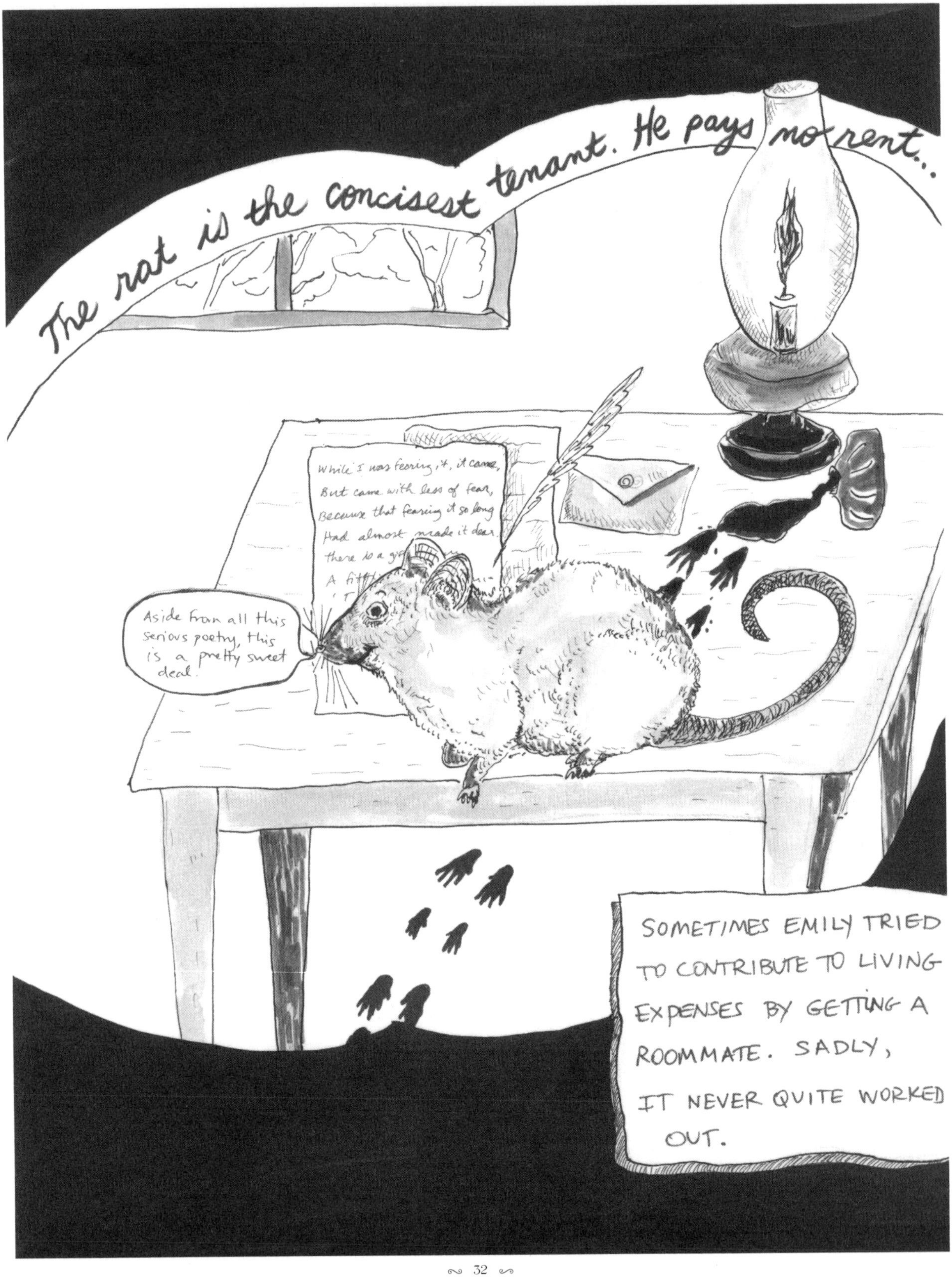

The rat is the concisest tenant. He pays no rent...
While I was fearing it, it came,
But came with less of fear,
Because that fearing it so long
Had almost made it dear.
Aside from all this serious poetry, this is a pretty sweet deal.
SOMETIMES EMILY TRIED TO CONTRIBUTE TO LIVING EXPENSES BY GETTING A ROOMMATE. SADLY, IT NEVER QUITE WORKED OUT.

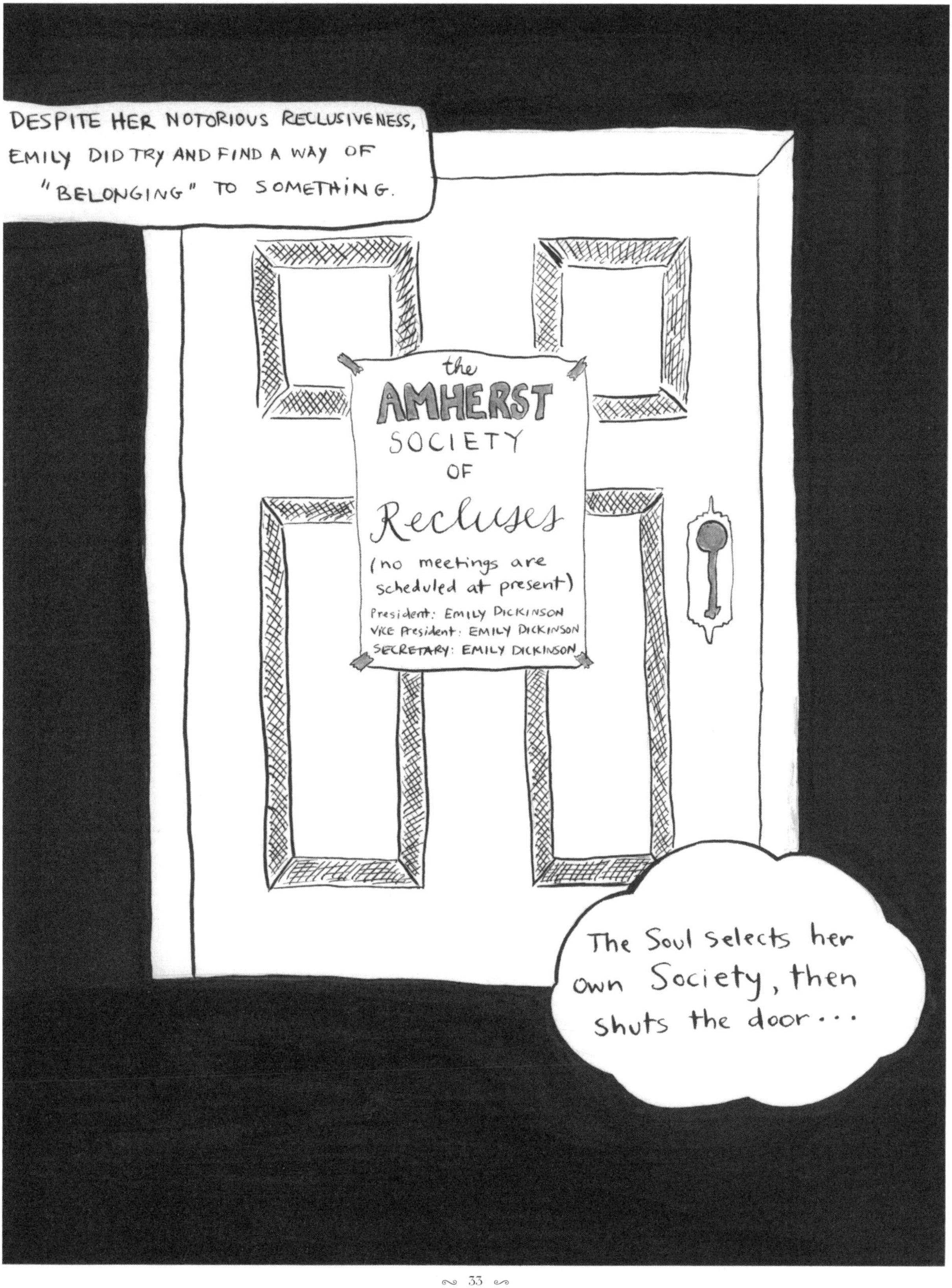
DESPITE HER NOTORIOUS RECLUSIVENESS, EMILY DID TRY AND FIND A WAY OF "BELONGING" TO SOMETHING.
the AMHERST SOCIETY OF Recluses
(no meetings are scheduled at present)
President: EMILY DICKINSON
VICE President: EMILY DICKINSON
SECRETARY: EMILY DICKINSON
The Soul selects her own Society, then shuts the door...

Dear Ms. Dickinson,

My daughter turned nine years old recently and I told her she could invite a small group of friends over to have cake and spend the night. In the early hours of the morning, I heard screams coming from her room. She was having a nightmare. It seems her friends told some ghost stories before retiring and they scared my daughter. She now has trouble sleeping through the night and she is convinced our house is haunted. What can I tell her to ease her mind? Signed, **Father Fear**

Dear **Father Fear,**

One need not be a chamber to be haunted,
One need not be a house;
The brain has corridors surpassing
Material place.

Far safer, of a midnight meeting
External ghost,
Than an interior confronting
That whiter host.

GAZETTE

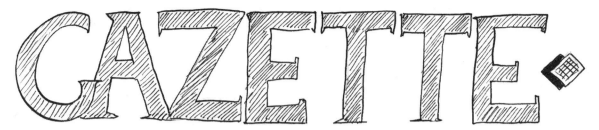

Dear Emily,

I recently lost my job and I have been having great difficulty finding another one. My wife is nagging me every night, as she is concerned about how we will pay our bills and feed our three children. My desk is piled with past-due bills and aside from food, we need winter coats and hats for everyone. Can you please tell me what I should do?

Yours, **Mr. Desperate**

Dear **Mr. Desperate,**

I meant to have but modest needs,
Such as content, and heaven;
Within my income these could lie,
And life and I keep even...

TOP CHEF Amherst!
I present to the judges my famous coconut cake. Father and brother Austin love this recipe. I added raspberry coulis and a fresh mint garnish ENJOY!
TOP CHEF
Emily was known for her baking abilities in her town, so she decided to branch out and try to appeal to a broader audience.
FAME IS A FICKLE FOOD UPON A SHIFTING PLATE...
hmmm, looks rather pedestrian, wouldn't you say?

DICKINZINE ~ ~ UNDERGROUND

(OR, UNDER BED?)

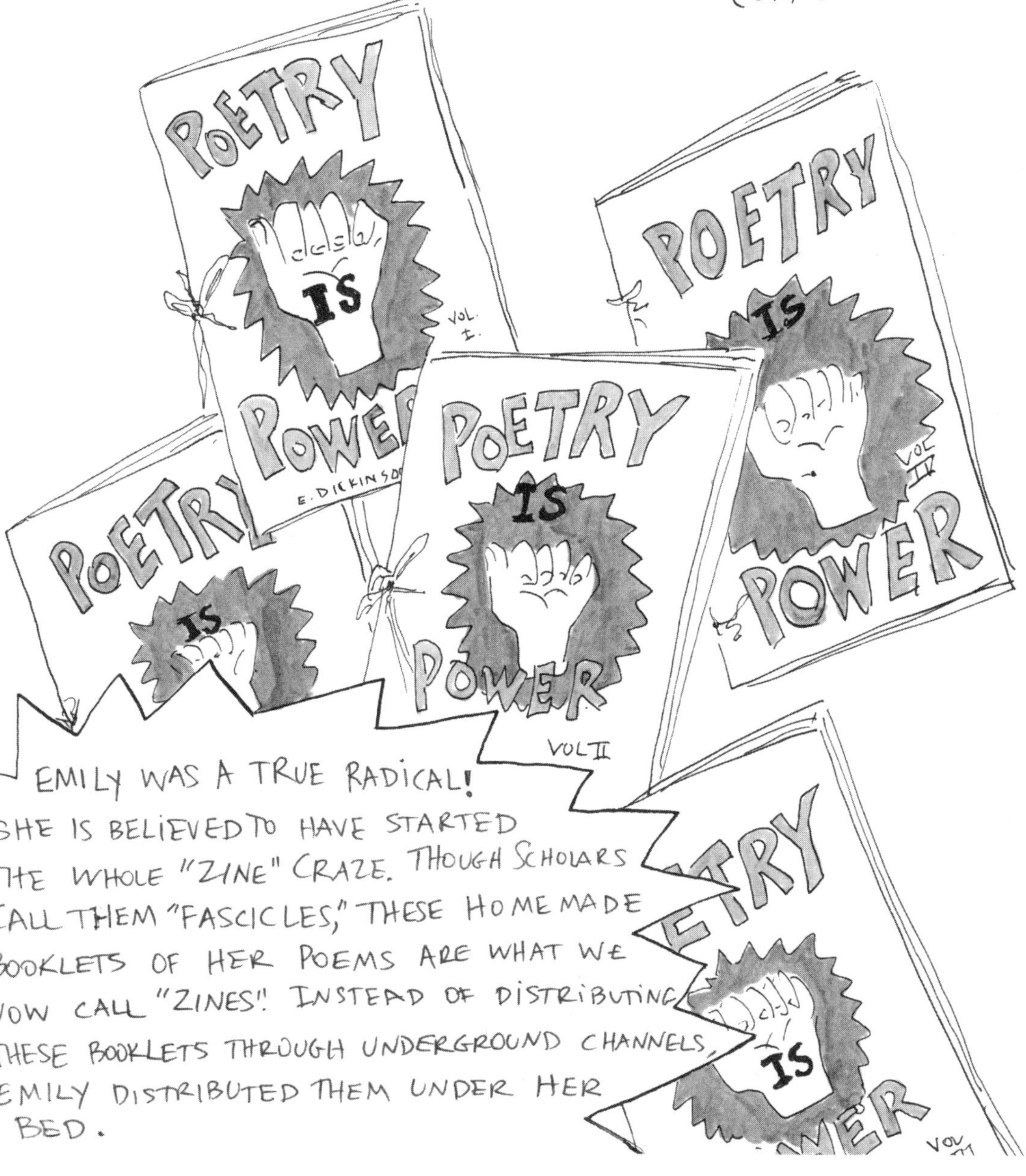

POETRY IS POWER
VOL. I.
E. DICKINSON
POETRY IS POWER
VOL IV
POETRY IS POWER
VOL II
POETRY IS

EMILY WAS A TRUE RADICAL! SHE IS BELIEVED TO HAVE STARTED THE WHOLE "ZINE" CRAZE. THOUGH SCHOLARS CALL THEM "FASCICLES," THESE HOMEMADE BOOKLETS OF HER POEMS ARE WHAT WE NOW CALL "ZINES!" INSTEAD OF DISTRIBUTING THESE BOOKLETS THROUGH UNDERGROUND CHANNELS, EMILY DISTRIBUTED THEM UNDER HER BED.

The ENVELOPE

In this short Life
that only lasts an hour
merely
How much – how
little – is
within our
power

Miss
Emily Dickinson
Amherst Mass

Was never
Frigate a
like

Kate's
Doughnuts
½ Cups Butter
2 Eggs
1 Cup Sugar
yeast
½ nutmeg
Salt
milk

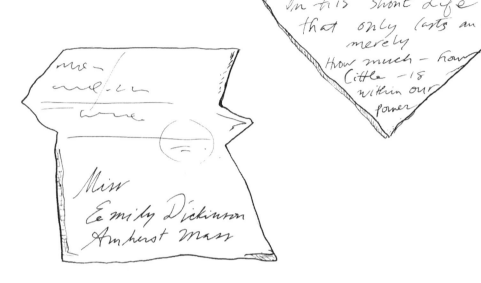

POEMS

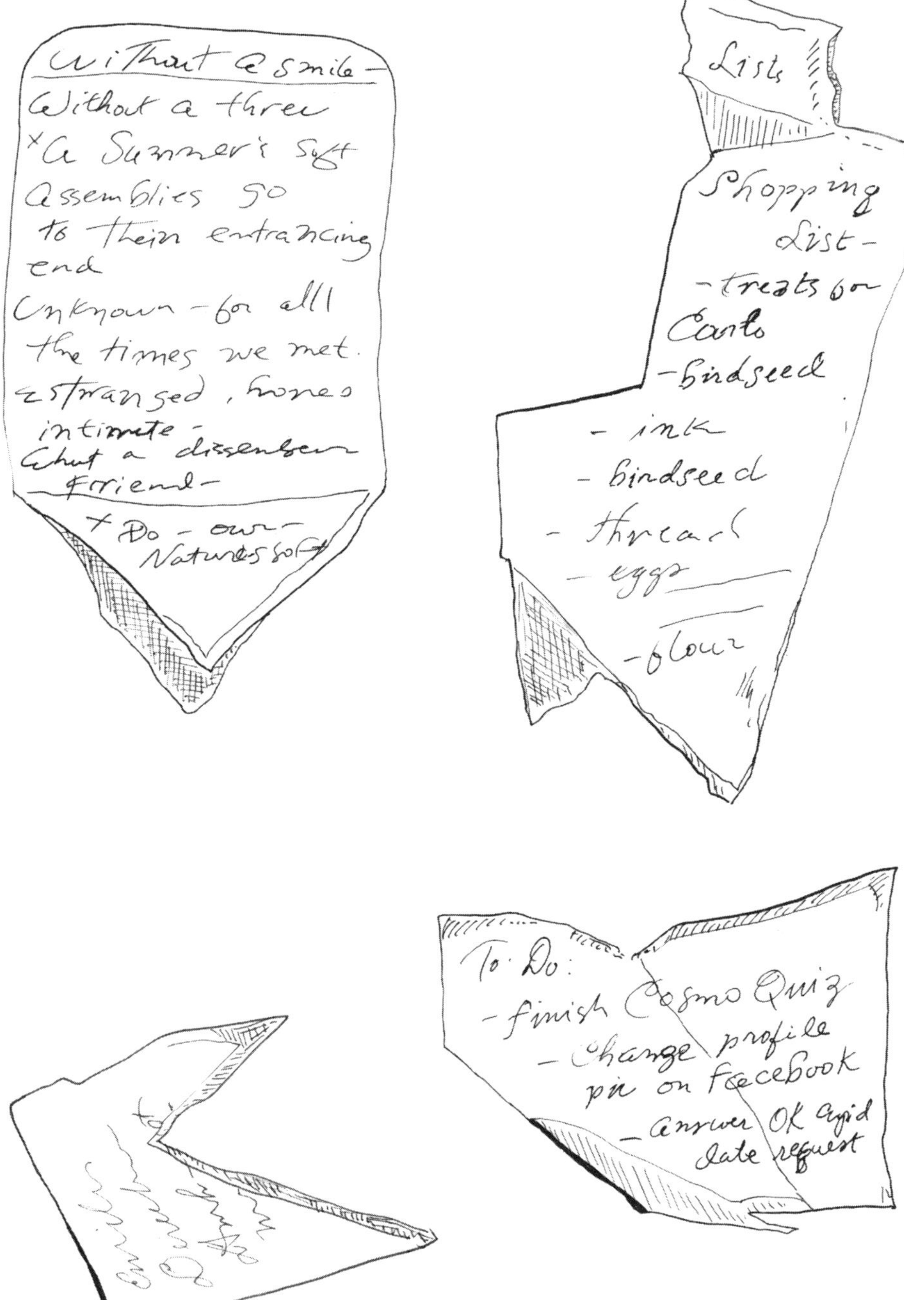

Without a smile —
Without a three
× A Summer's soft
Assemblies go
to their entrancing
end
Unknown — for all
the times we met.
estranged, hones
intimate —
What a dissenbenn
— Friend —

× Do — our —
Natures soft

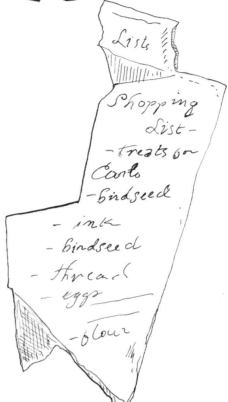

Lists

Shopping
List —
— treats for
Carlo
— birdseed

— ink

— birdseed

— thread

— eggs

— flour

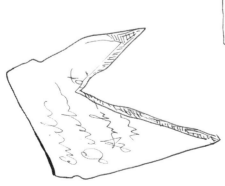

To Do:
— finish Cosmo Quiz
— change profile
pic on Facebook
— answer OK cupid
date request

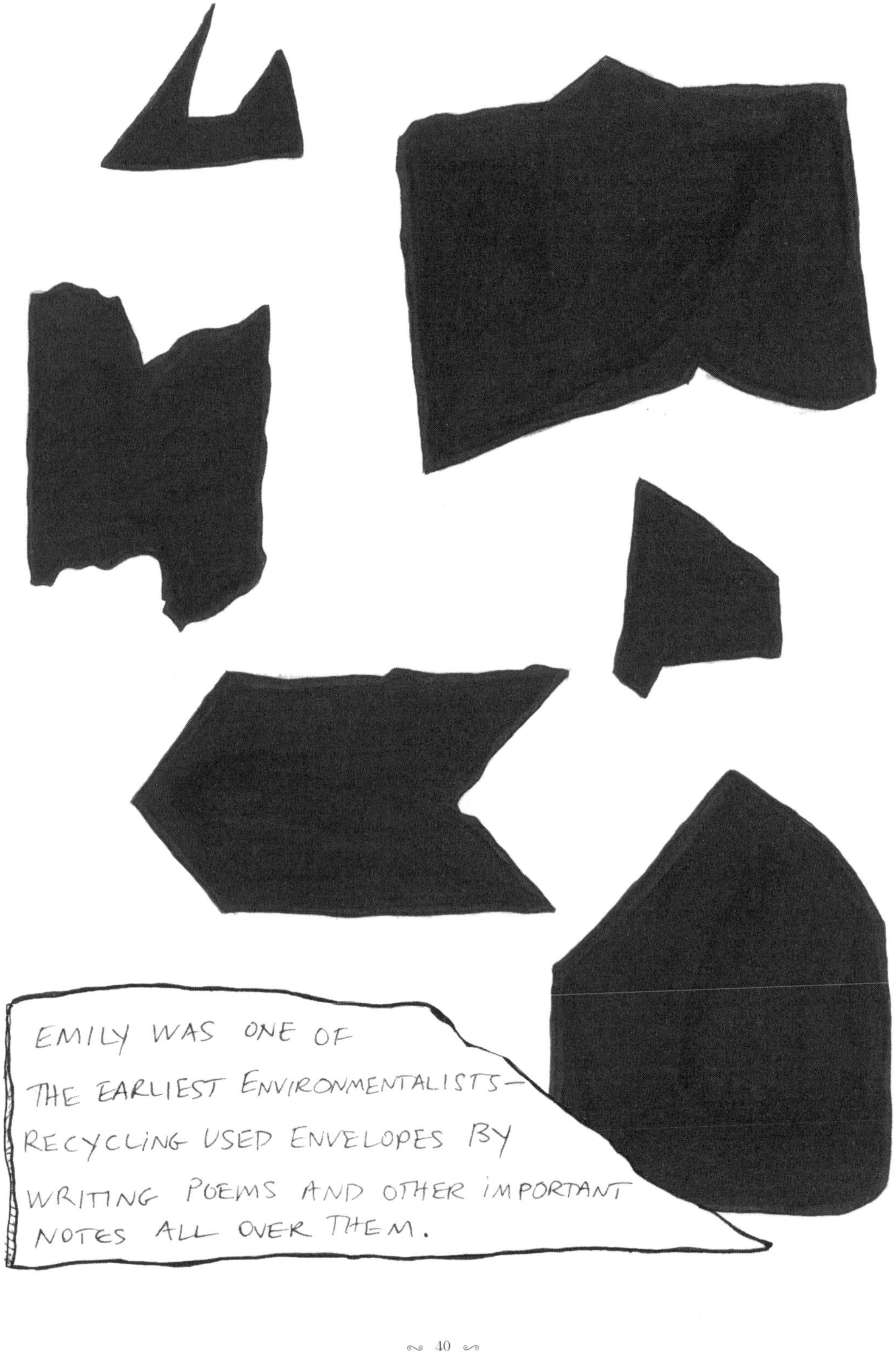
EMILY WAS ONE OF
THE EARLIEST ENVIRONMENTALISTS—
RECYCLING USED ENVELOPES BY
WRITING POEMS AND OTHER IMPORTANT
NOTES ALL OVER THEM.

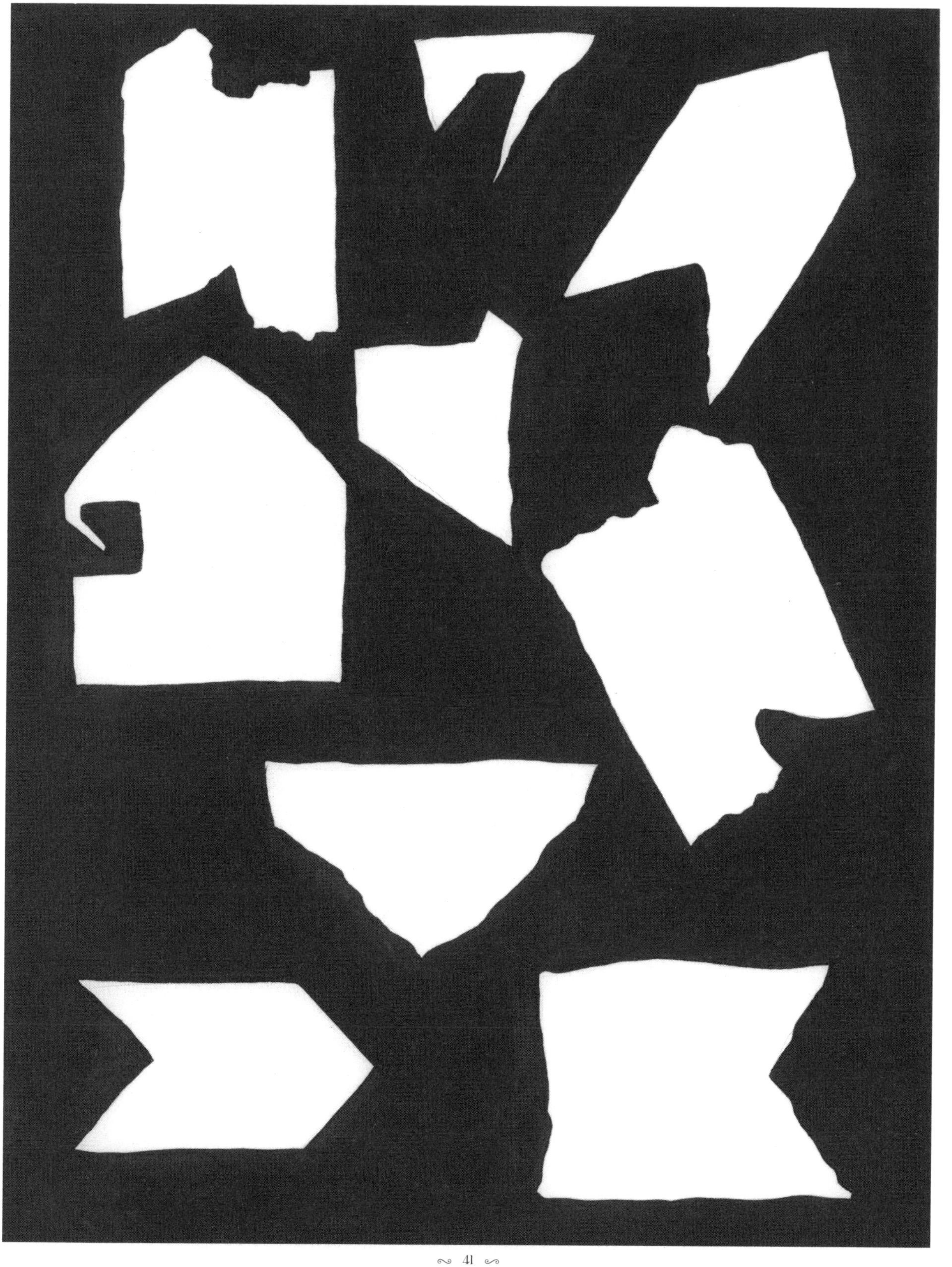

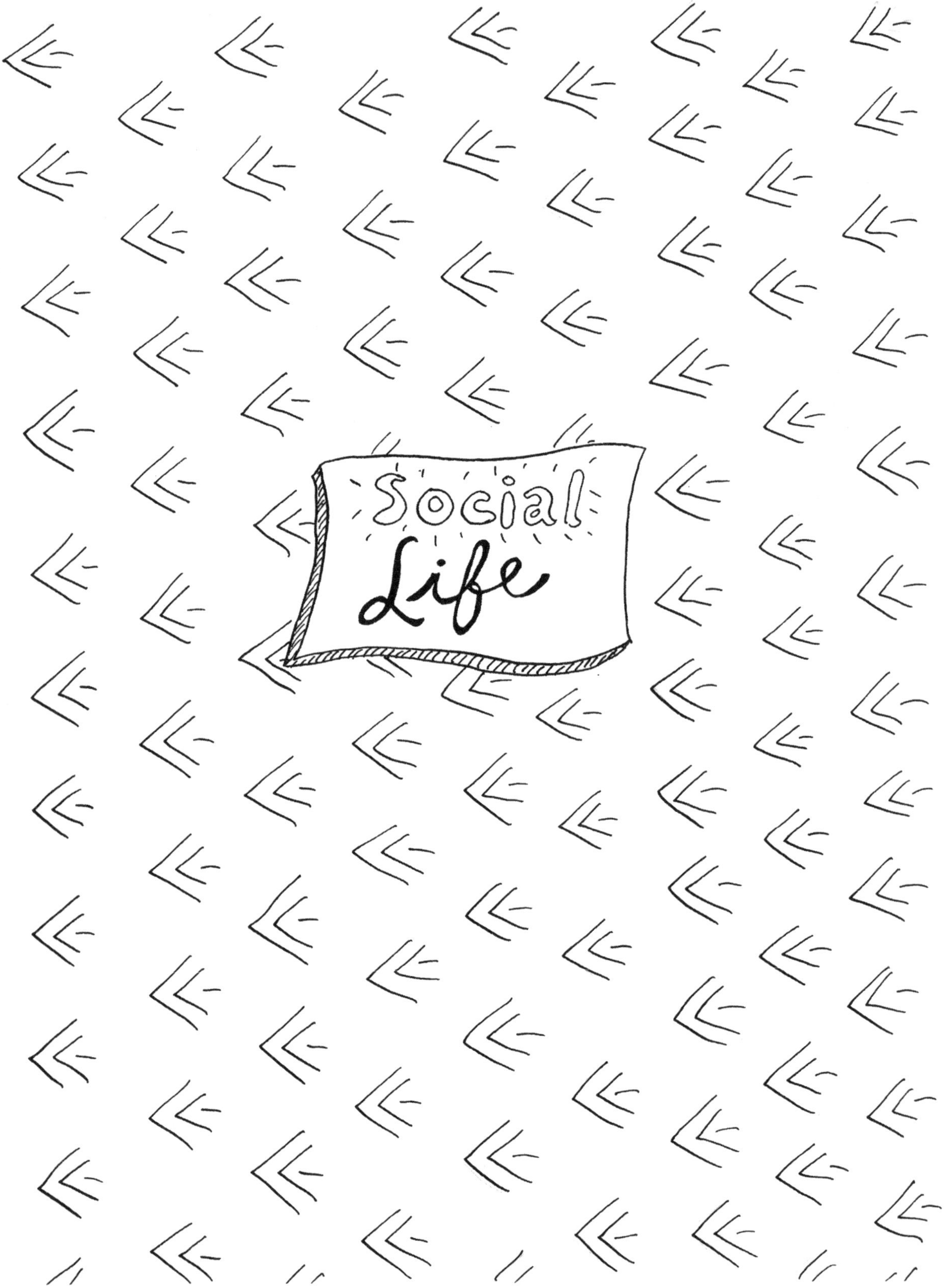
Social
Life

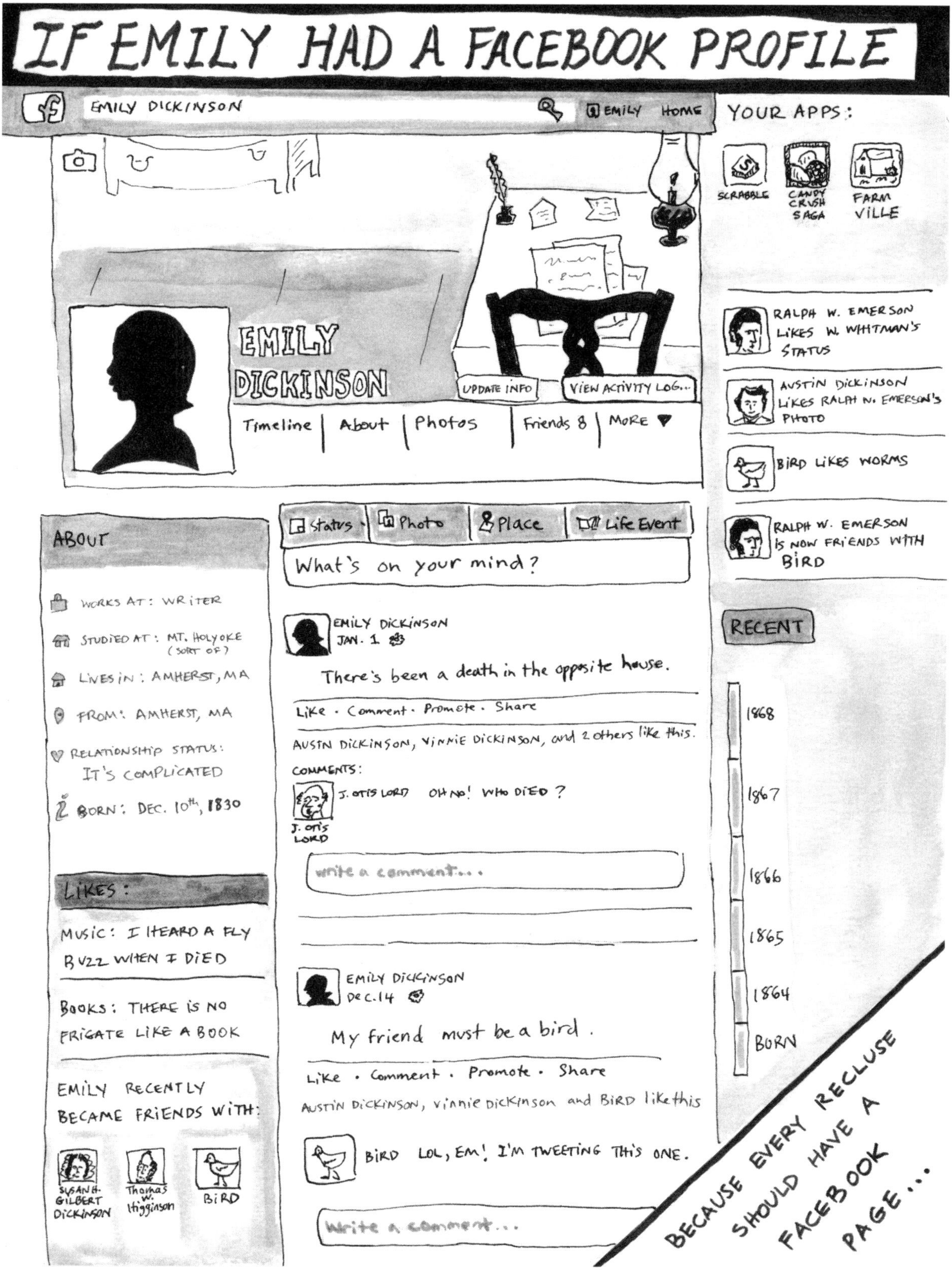
IF EMILY HAD A FACEBOOK PROFILE
EMILY DICKINSON
EMILY
HOME
YOUR APPS:
SCRABBLE
CANDY CRUSH SAGA
FARM VILLE
EMILY DICKINSON
UPDATE INFO
VIEW ACTIVITY LOG...
Timeline
About
Photos
Friends 8
MORE
RALPH W. EMERSON LIKES W. WHITMAN'S STATUS
AUSTIN DICKINSON LIKES RALPH W. EMERSON'S PHOTO
BIRD LIKES WORMS
RALPH W. EMERSON IS NOW FRIENDS WITH BIRD
ABOUT
WORKS AT: WRITER
STUDIED AT: MT. HOLYOKE (SORT OF)
LIVES IN: AMHERST, MA
FROM: AMHERST, MA
RELATIONSHIP STATUS: IT'S COMPLICATED
BORN: DEC. 10th, 1830
Status
Photo
Place
Life Event
What's on your mind?
EMILY DICKINSON
JAN. 1
There's been a death in the opposite house.
Like · Comment · Promote · Share
AUSTIN DICKINSON, VINNIE DICKINSON, and 2 others like this.
COMMENTS:
J. OTIS LORD OH NO! WHO DIED?
J. OTIS LORD
write a comment...
RECENT
1868
1867
1866
1865
1864
BORN
LIKES:
MUSIC: I HEARD A FLY BUZZ WHEN I DIED
BOOKS: THERE IS NO FRIGATE LIKE A BOOK
EMILY RECENTLY BECAME FRIENDS WITH:
SUSAN H. GILBERT DICKINSON
Thomas W. Higginson
BIRD
EMILY DICKINSON
DEC. 14
My friend must be a bird.
Like · Comment · Promote · Share
AUSTIN DICKINSON, VINNIE DICKINSON and BIRD like this
BIRD LOL, EM! I'M TWEETING THIS ONE.
Write a comment...
BECAUSE EVERY RECLUSE SHOULD HAVE A FACEBOOK PAGE...

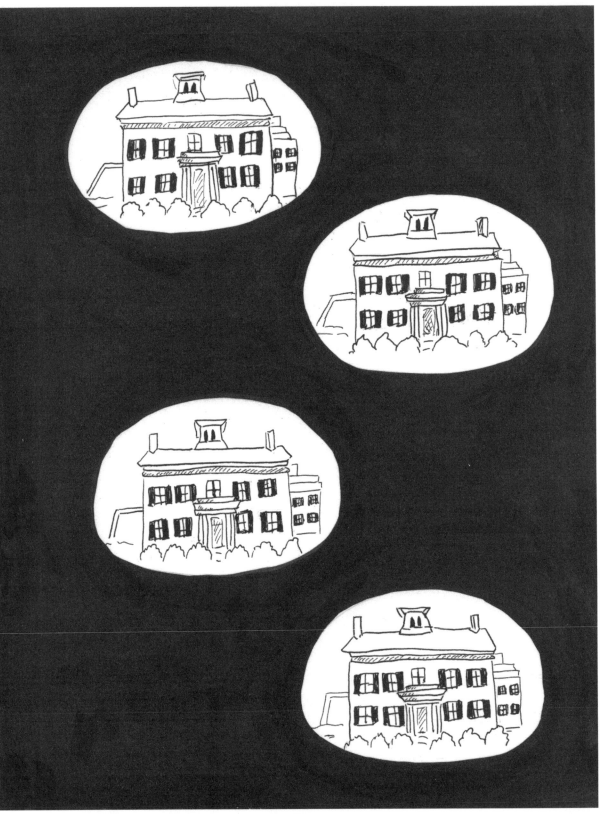

I taste a liquor never brewed...
EMILY WAS KNOWN TO KNOCK A FEW BACK WHEN THE WRITING BECAME A LITTLE DIFFICULT.
ABSOLUT
Limited Edition
RECLUSE
"I shall but drink the more!"
E. Dickinson
40% ALC./VOL. (80 PROOF) 1 LITER
IMPORTED

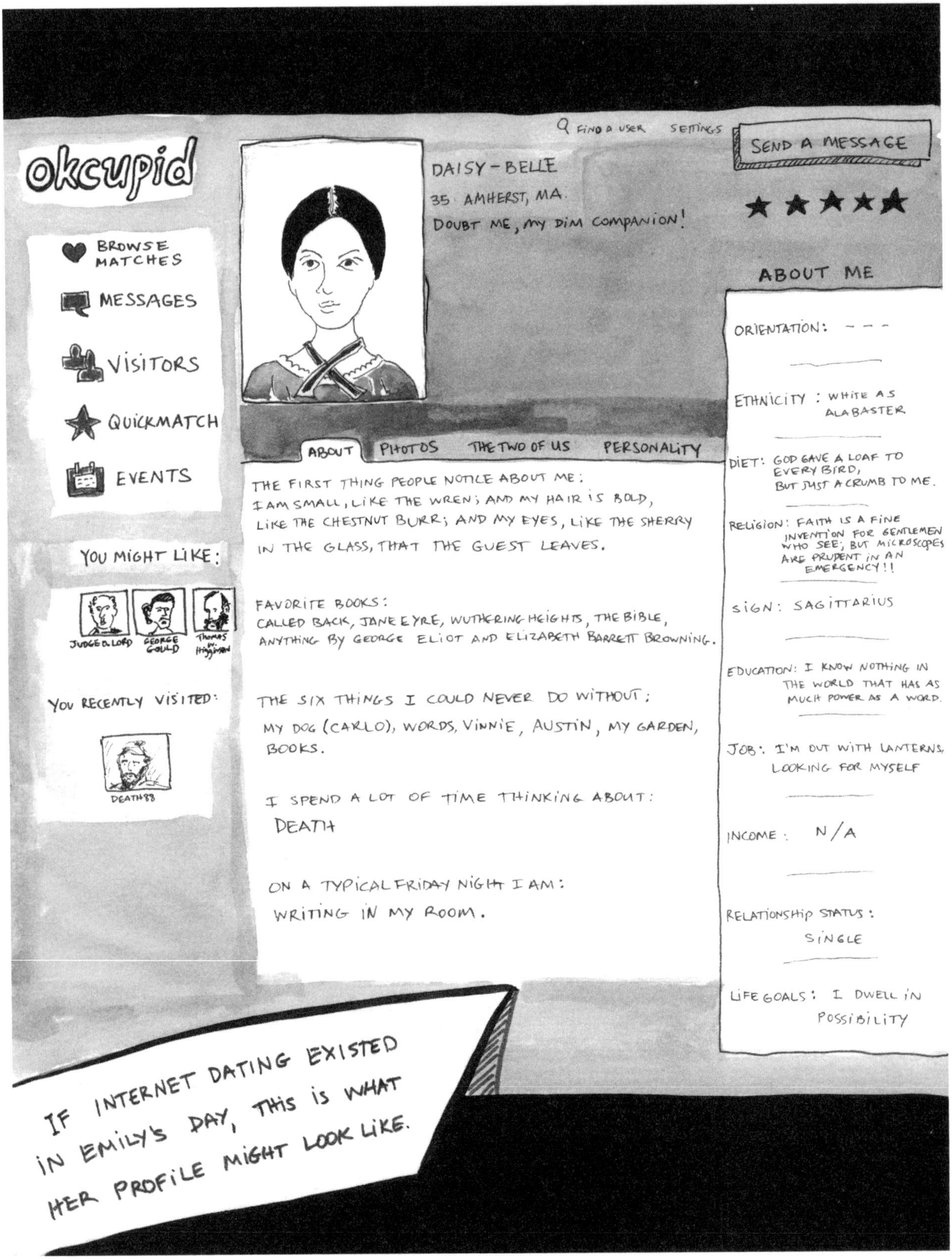
okcupid
FIND A USER
SETTINGS
SEND A MESSAGE
DAISY-BELLE
35 AMHERST, MA.
DOUBT ME, MY DIM COMPANION!
BROWSE MATCHES
MESSAGES
VISITORS
QUICKMATCH
EVENTS
YOU MIGHT LIKE:
JUDGE O. LORD
GEORGE GOULD
Thomas W. Higginson
YOU RECENTLY VISITED:
DEATH88
ABOUT
PHOTOS
THE TWO OF US
PERSONALITY
THE FIRST THING PEOPLE NOTICE ABOUT ME:
I AM SMALL, LIKE THE WREN; AND MY HAIR IS BOLD, LIKE THE CHESTNUT BURR; AND MY EYES, LIKE THE SHERRY IN THE GLASS, THAT THE GUEST LEAVES.
FAVORITE BOOKS:
CALLED BACK, JANE EYRE, WUTHERING HEIGHTS, THE BIBLE, ANYTHING BY GEORGE ELIOT AND ELIZABETH BARRETT BROWNING.
THE SIX THINGS I COULD NEVER DO WITHOUT:
MY DOG (CARLO), WORDS, VINNIE, AUSTIN, MY GARDEN, BOOKS.
I SPEND A LOT OF TIME THINKING ABOUT:
DEATH
ON A TYPICAL FRIDAY NIGHT I AM:
WRITING IN MY ROOM.
ABOUT ME
ORIENTATION: - - -
ETHNICITY: WHITE AS ALABASTER
DIET: GOD GAVE A LOAF TO EVERY BIRD, BUT JUST A CRUMB TO ME.
RELIGION: FAITH IS A FINE INVENTION FOR GENTLEMEN WHO SEE; BUT MICROSCOPES ARE PRUDENT IN AN EMERGENCY!!
SIGN: SAGITTARIUS
EDUCATION: I KNOW NOTHING IN THE WORLD THAT HAS AS MUCH POWER AS A WORD.
JOB: I'M OUT WITH LANTERNS, LOOKING FOR MYSELF
INCOME: N/A
RELATIONSHIP STATUS: SINGLE
LIFE GOALS: I DWELL IN POSSIBILITY
IF INTERNET DATING EXISTED IN EMILY'S DAY, THIS IS WHAT HER PROFILE MIGHT LOOK LIKE.

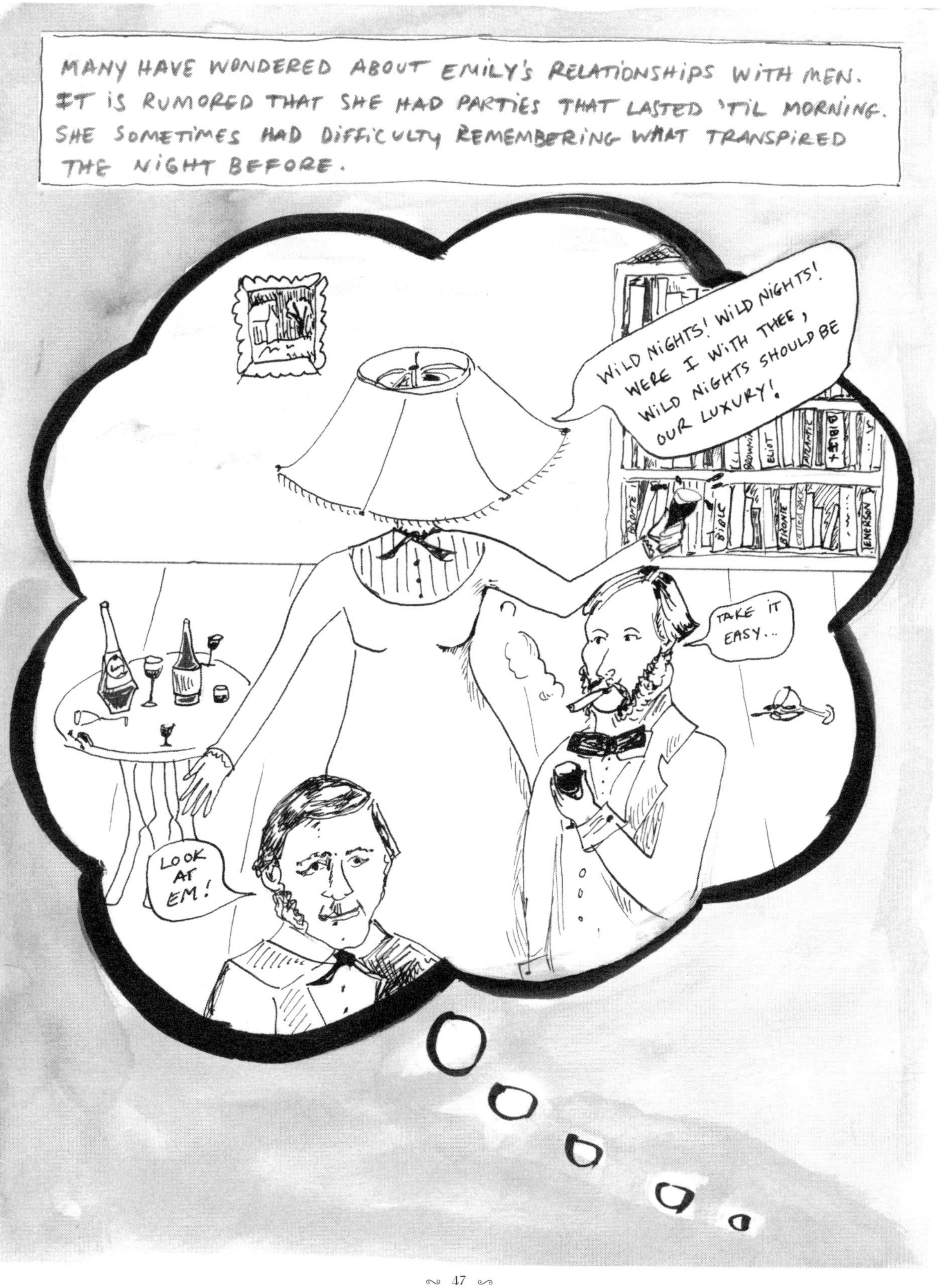
MANY HAVE WONDERED ABOUT EMILY'S RELATIONSHIPS WITH MEN. IT IS RUMORED THAT SHE HAD PARTIES THAT LASTED 'TIL MORNING. SHE SOMETIMES HAD DIFFICULTY REMEMBERING WHAT TRANSPIRED THE NIGHT BEFORE.
WILD NIGHTS! WILD NIGHTS! WERE I WITH THEE, WILD NIGHTS SHOULD BE OUR LUXURY!
TAKE IT EASY...
LOOK AT EM!

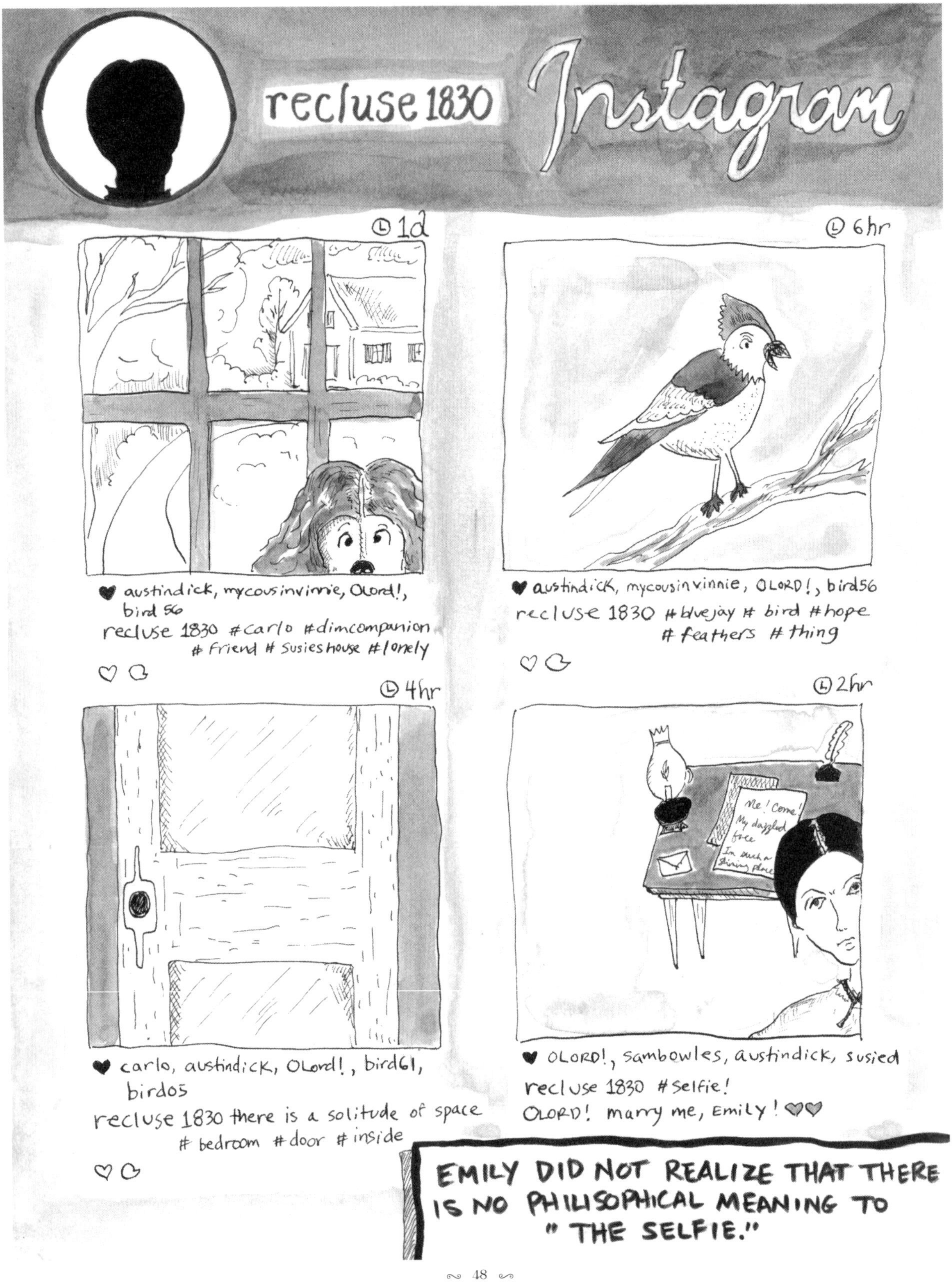
recluse 1830
Instagram
1d
austindick, mycousinvinnie, OLord!, bird 56
recluse 1830 #carlo #dimcompanion #friend #susieshouse #lonely
6hr
austindick, mycousinvinnie, OLORD!, bird56
recluse 1830 #bluejay #bird #hope #feathers #thing
4hr
carlo, austindick, OLord!, bird61, birdo5
recluse 1830 there is a solitude of space #bedroom #door #inside
2hr
Me! Come! My dazzled face In such a shining place
OLORD!, sambowles, austindick, susied
recluse 1830 #selfie!
OLORD! marry me, Emily!
EMILY DID NOT REALIZE THAT THERE IS NO PHILISOPHICAL MEANING TO "THE SELFIE."

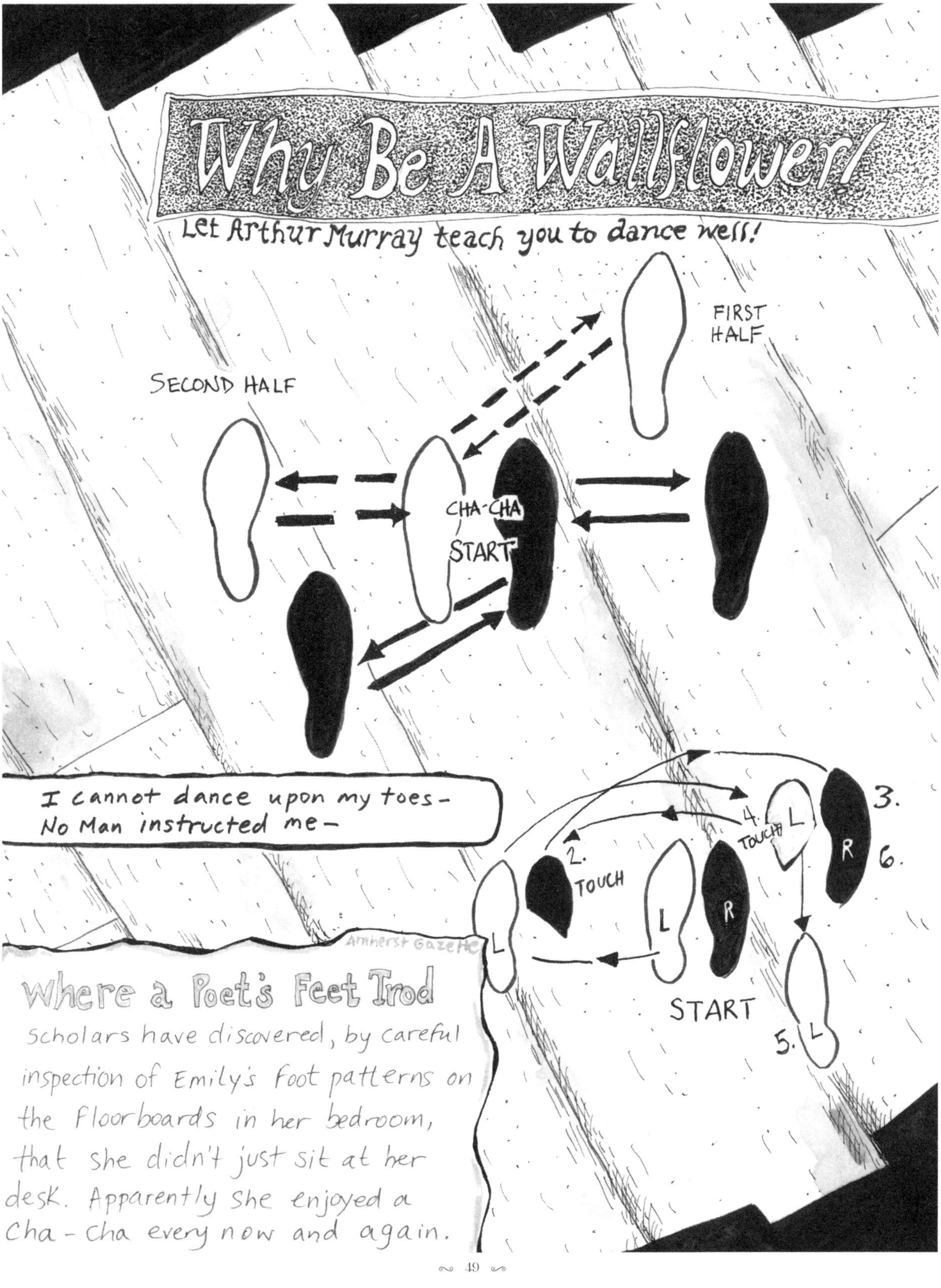

Why Be A Wallflower!

Let Arthur Murray teach you to dance well!

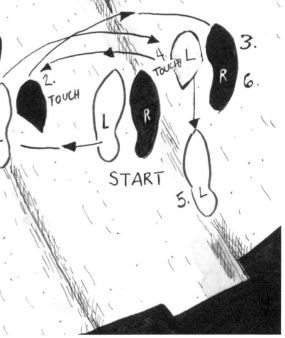

FIRST HALF

SECOND HALF

CHA-CHA
START

> I cannot dance upon my toes—
> No Man instructed me—

2. TOUCH

4. TOUCH

3.

6.

5. L

L

R

L

R

START

Amherst Gazette

Where a Poet's Feet Trod

Scholars have discovered, by careful inspection of Emily's foot patterns on the floorboards in her bedroom, that she didn't just sit at her desk. Apparently she enjoyed a Cha-Cha every now and again.

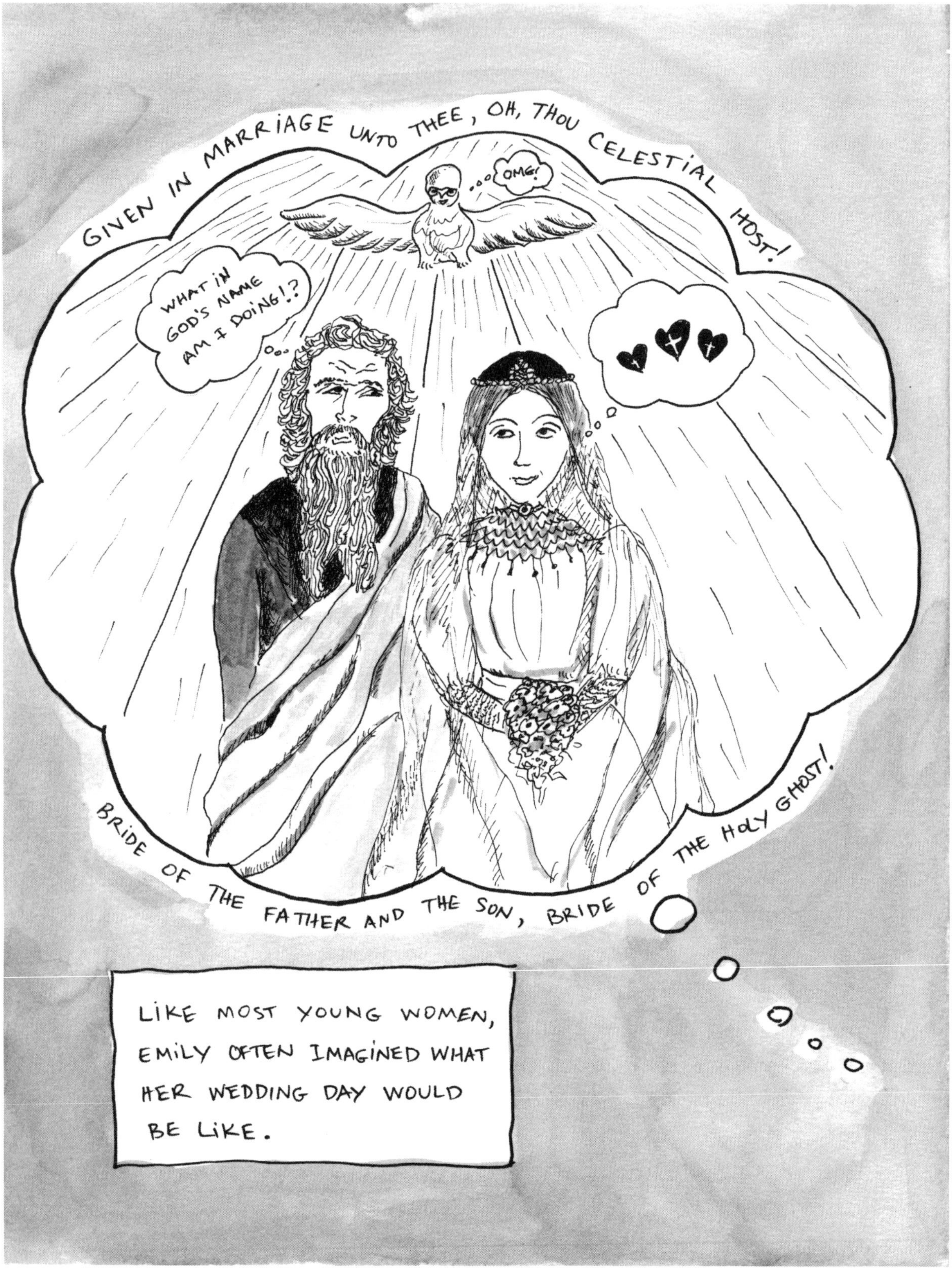
GIVEN IN MARRIAGE UNTO THEE, OH, THOU CELESTIAL HOST!
OMG!
WHAT IN GOD'S NAME AM I DOING!?
BRIDE OF THE FATHER AND THE SON, BRIDE OF THE HOLY GHOST!
LIKE MOST YOUNG WOMEN, EMILY OFTEN IMAGINED WHAT HER WEDDING DAY WOULD BE LIKE.

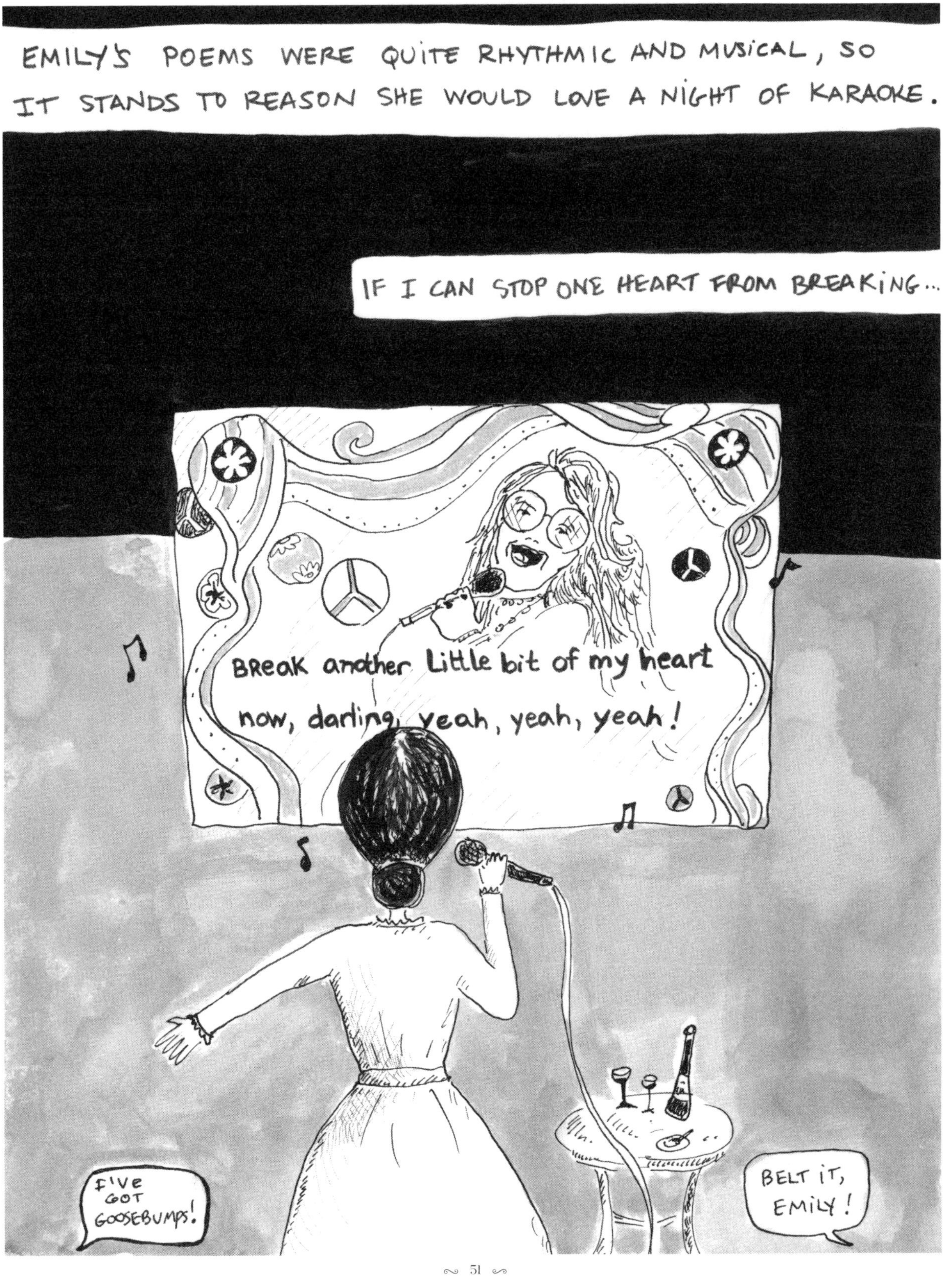
EMILY'S POEMS WERE QUITE RHYTHMIC AND MUSICAL, SO IT STANDS TO REASON SHE WOULD LOVE A NIGHT OF KARAOKE.
IF I CAN STOP ONE HEART FROM BREAKING...
Break another Little bit of my heart now, darling, yeah, yeah, yeah!
I'VE GOT GOOSEBUMPS!
BELT IT, EMILY!

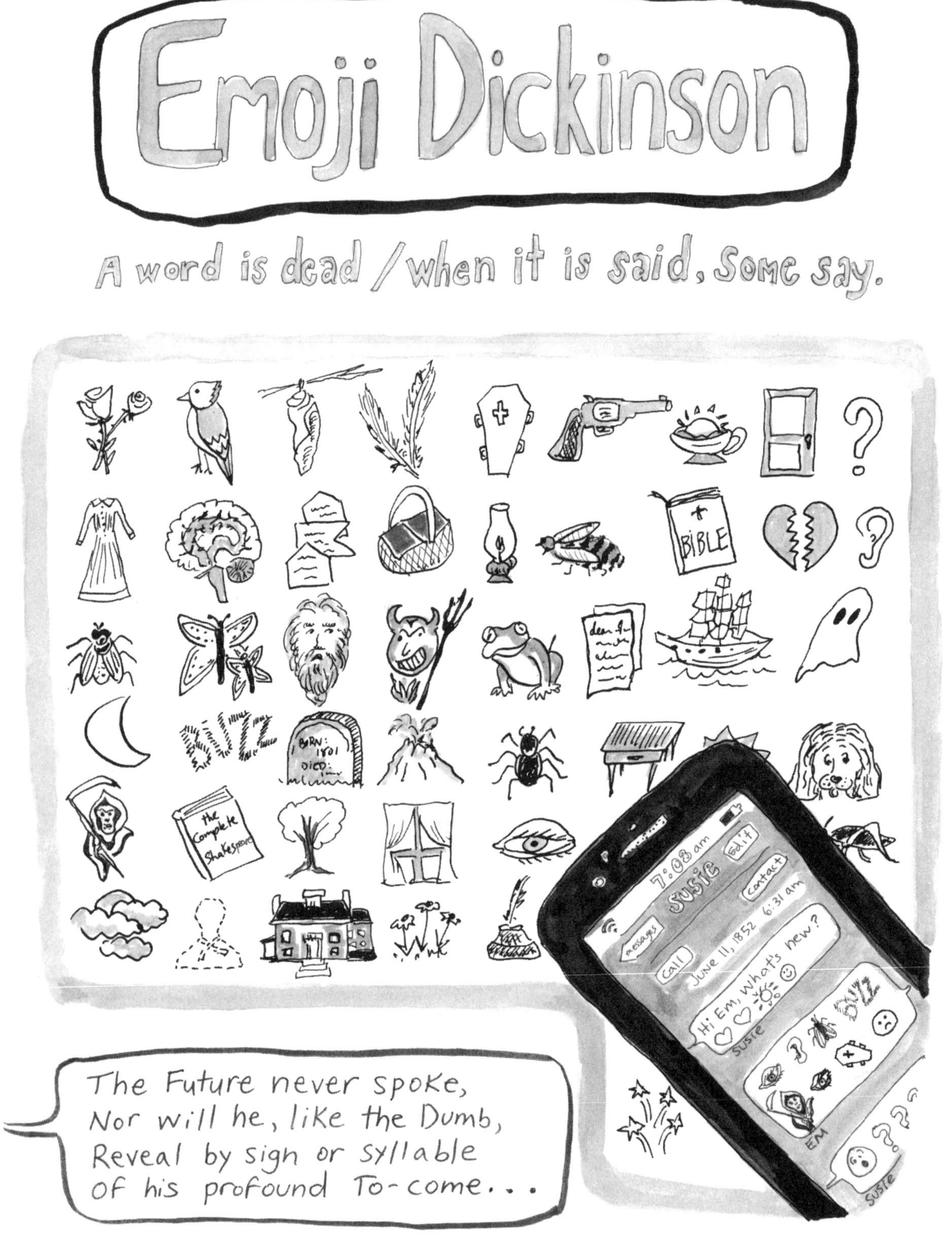

Emoji Dickinson
A word is dead / when it is said, Some say.
BIBLE
BUZZ
BORN: 1801 DIED:
the Complete Shakespeare
7:08 am
Edit
SUSIE
messages
Contact
Call
June 11, 1852 6:31 am
Hi Em, what's new?
SUSIE
EM
SUSIE
The Future never spoke,
Nor will he, like the Dumb,
Reveal by sign or syllable
Of his profound To-come...

EMILY'S favorite acronyms

ROTFL: robins offer the finest lullabies

TBD: thinking 'bout death

FOMO: fear of meeting outside

LOL: listening on landing

WTF: where's that fly?

ASAP: a skeptic's approach to prayer

ADIDAD: all day I dream about death

LMAO: love my amazing ornithology

WFM: words fill me

BFF: bird friends forever

MMW: my meter wavers

BTW: by the window

TBA: to be alive

NP: no people

BS: birds singing

FAQ: faith and questions

OMG: Oh my God!

OT: oppressing thoughts

AS SOMEONE WHO WROTE
THOUSANDS OF LETTERS,
EMILY SOMETIMES
RESORTED TO ACRONYMS
TO SAVE TIME.

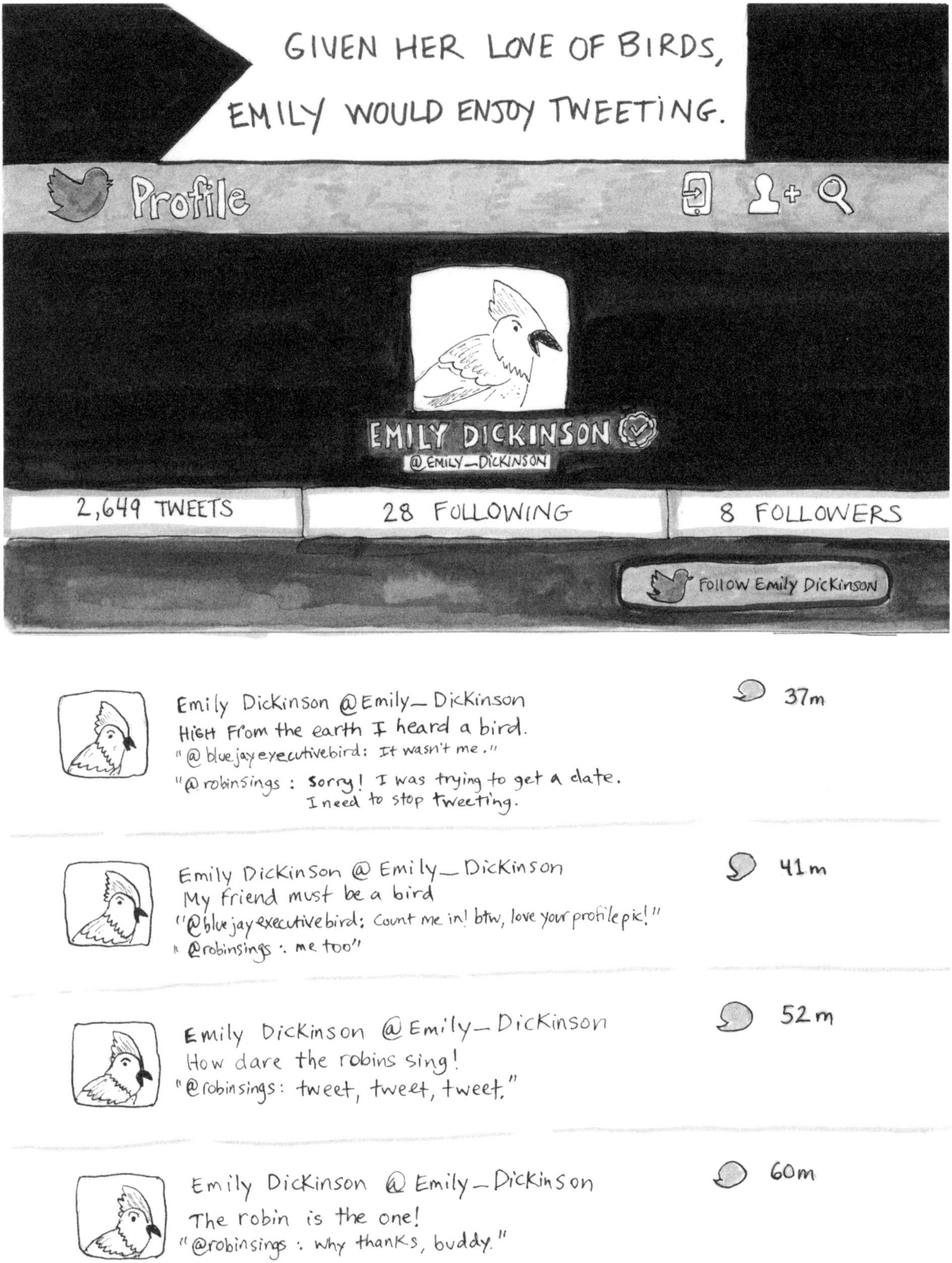

GIVEN HER LOVE OF BIRDS,
EMILY WOULD ENJOY TWEETING.

 Profile

EMILY DICKINSON
@EMILY_DICKINSON

| 2,649 TWEETS | 28 FOLLOWING | 8 FOLLOWERS |

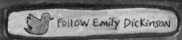 Follow Emily Dickinson

---

 Emily Dickinson @Emily_Dickinson   37m
High from the earth I heard a bird.
"@bluejayexecutivebird: It wasn't me."
"@robinsings : Sorry! I was trying to get a date.
     I need to stop tweeting.

 Emily Dickinson @ Emily_Dickinson   41m
My friend must be a bird
"@bluejayexecutivebird: Count me in! btw, love your profile pic!"
" @robinsings :. me too"

 Emily Dickinson @Emily_Dickinson   52m
How dare the robins sing!
"@robinsings: tweet, tweet, tweet."

 Emily Dickinson @ Emily_Dickinson   60m
The robin is the one!
"@robinsings : why thanks, buddy."

Emily Dickinson's Apps

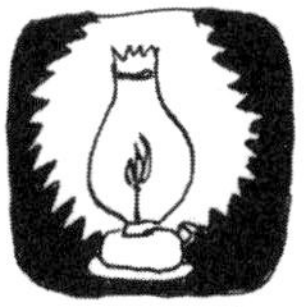

The Brightest Lantern

"We grow accustomed to the dark- when light is put away." Sure, you may grow accustomed to the Dark, But now you don't have to! Just click on the BrIGHTEST Lantern to Light your way!

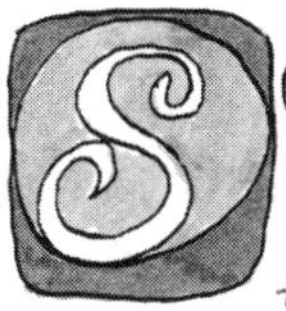

Spinsterest

The App that connects you with the world's Largest Spinster network! You're not Alone! Enter your personal dating history to find out if you are the "Spinsterest" of them all.

"The Soul unto itself Is an imperial friend."

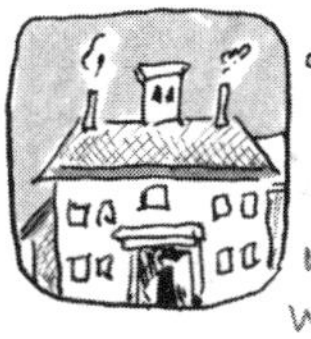

Home-Steady

Not used to leaving the Home Stead? Worried that you may lose your way Back? This indispensable App Guides you Back to the HOMESTEAD FROM THE VERY Moment you step out the door!

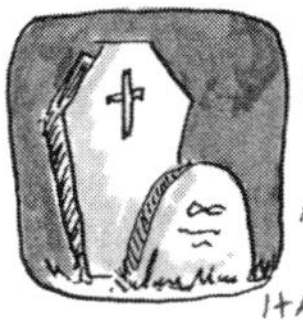

iDie™

"IT WAS NOT DEATH, FOR I STOOD Up."

HAVE YOU EVER IMAGINED YOUR OWN DEATH? MAYBE FOR THE purpose of creative expression? iDie™ offers thousands of possible expiration Scenarios! (Perfect companion to iBUZZ-the App for sound effects in the afterlife)

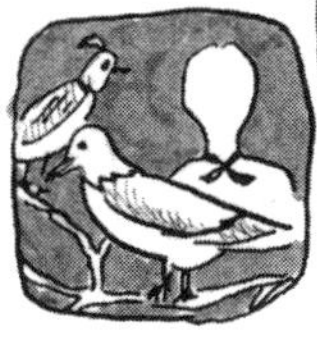

Birds with friends

"My friend must be a bird."

Feeling lonely? Having a hard time finding friends who communicate on your level? Birds with friends™ connects you with a huge network of birds! Robins, blue jays, sparrows - they're all waiting to hear from you.

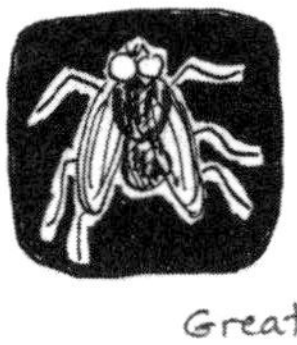

iBUZZ!!™

"I heard a fly buzz when I died."

Great when synced with iDie™, this app provides you with thousands of SOUND effects of the afterlife. Whether it be a buzzing fly (the #1 sound heard at the time of death) or the song of a robin - this app has it all!

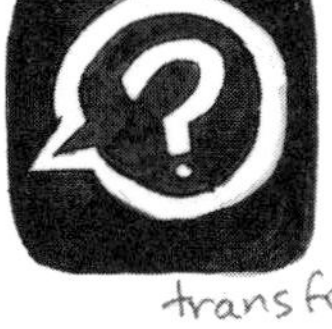

What's Apt?

Do you often get the urge to write uncomfortably passionate missives to your sister-in-law? Before you do, run them through What's Apt?™ and they will be transformed into more appropriate expressions.

"... I add a Kiss, shyly, lest there is somebody there! Don't let them see, will you Susie?"

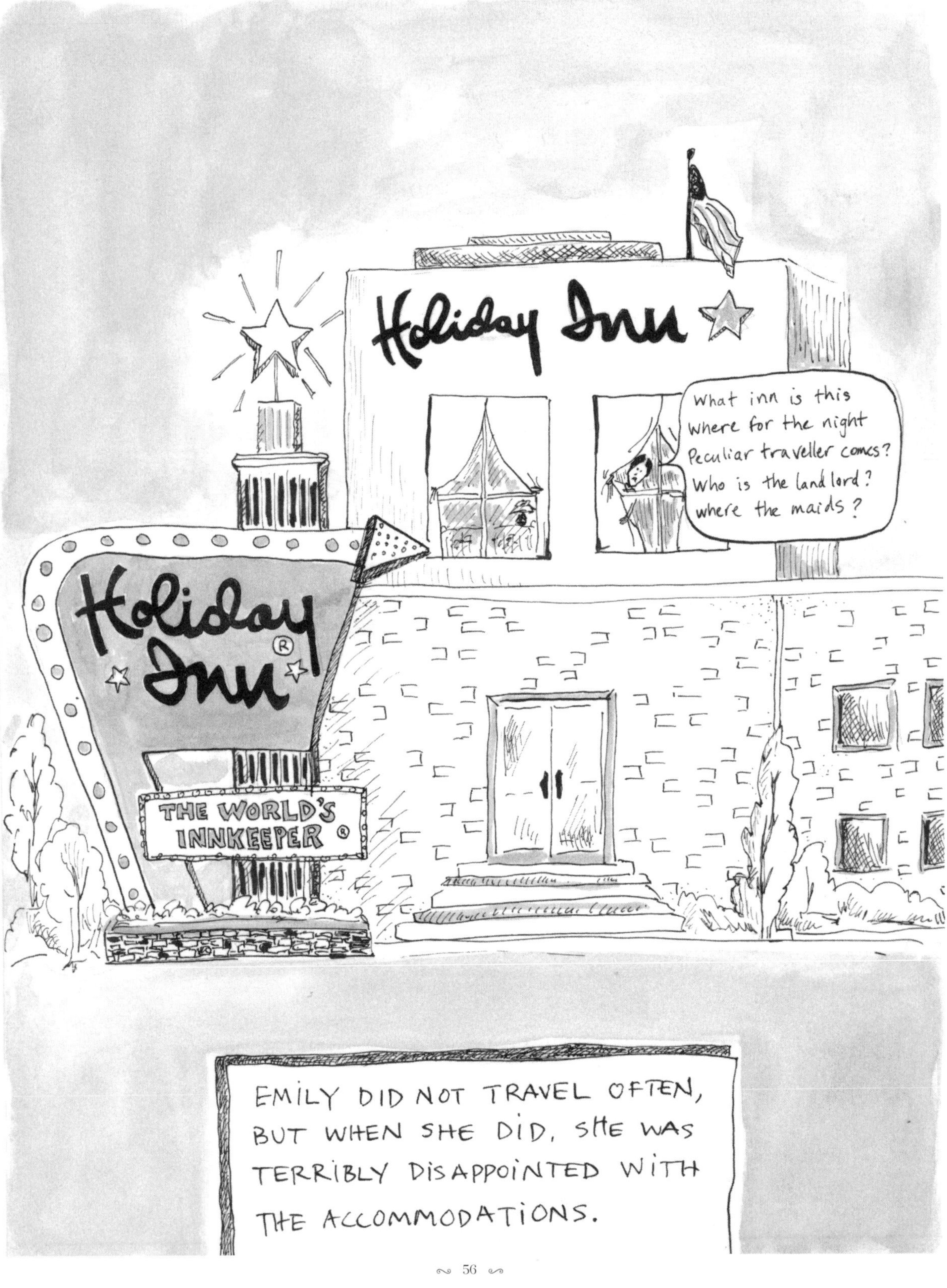
Holiday Inn
What inn is this
where for the night
Peculiar traveller comes?
Who is the landlord?
where the maids?
Holiday Inn ®
THE WORLD'S INNKEEPER ®
EMILY DID NOT TRAVEL OFTEN, BUT WHEN SHE DID, SHE WAS TERRIBLY DISAPPOINTED WITH THE ACCOMMODATIONS.

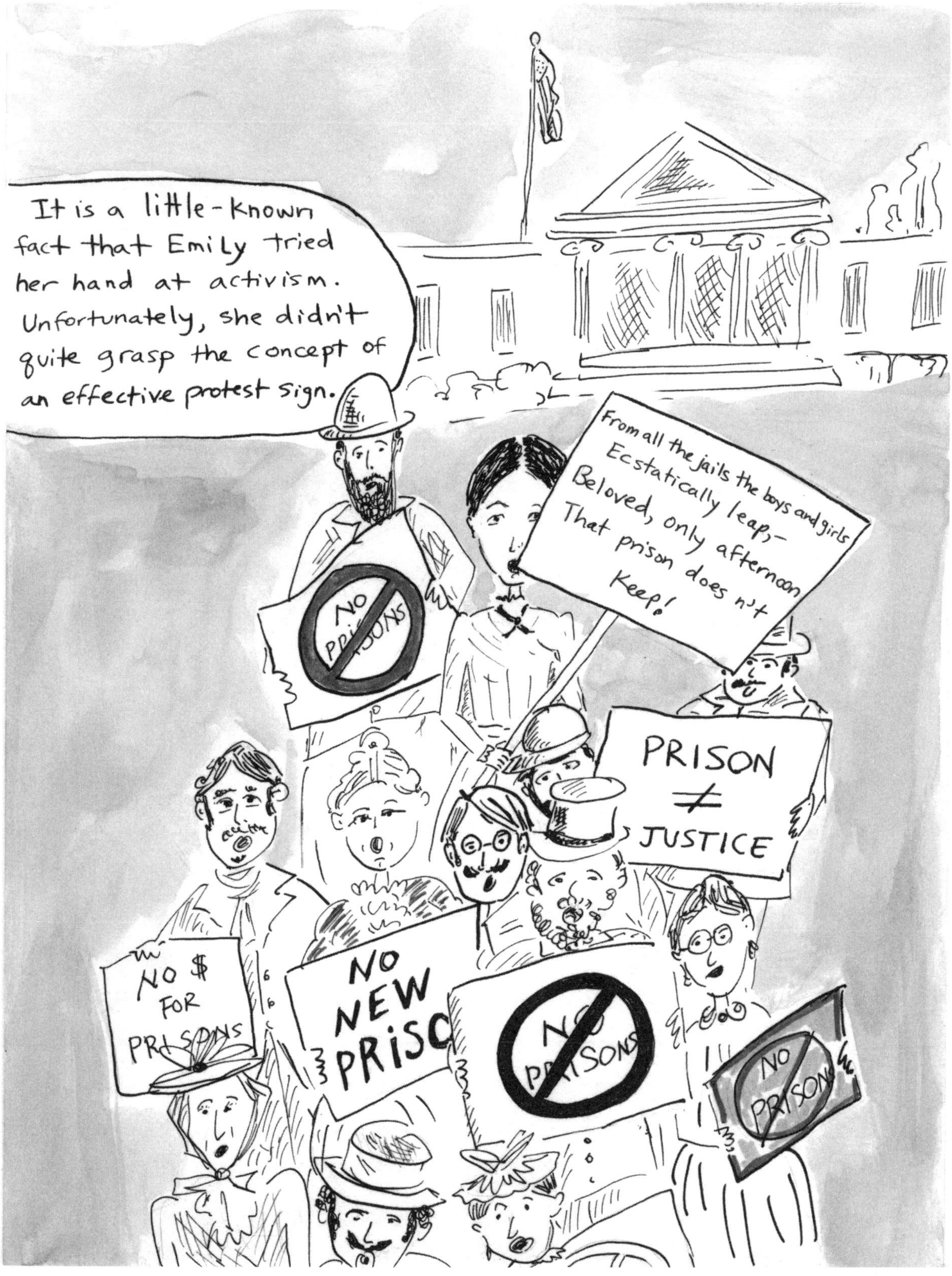
It is a little-known fact that Emily tried her hand at activism. Unfortunately, she didn't quite grasp the concept of an effective protest sign.
From all the jails the boys and girls Ecstatically leap,— Beloved, only afternoon That prison doesn't keep!
NO PRISONS
PRISON ≠ JUSTICE
NO $ FOR PRISONS
NO NEW PRISO
NO PRISONS
NO PRISONS

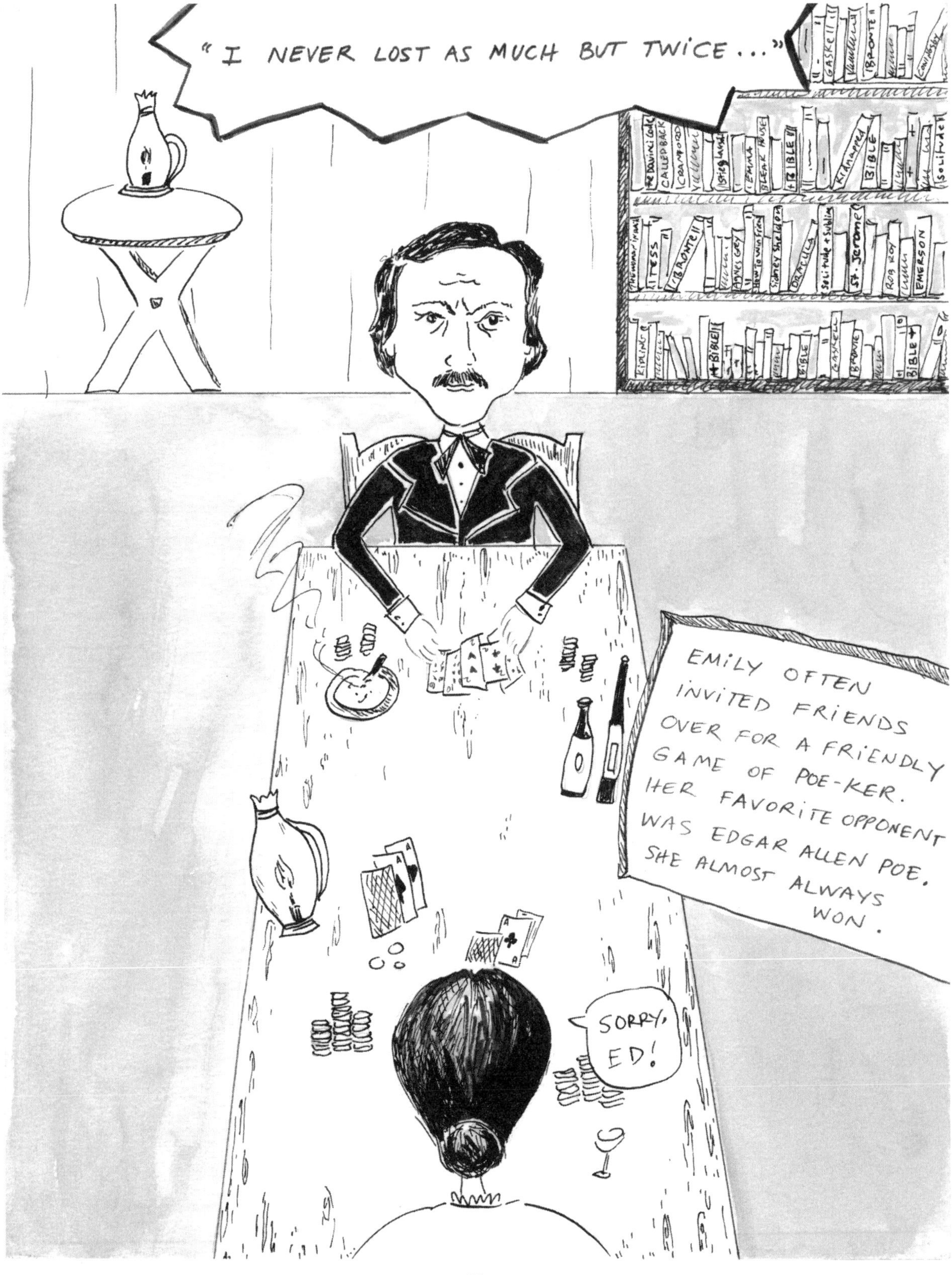
"I NEVER LOST AS MUCH BUT TWICE..."
EMILY OFTEN INVITED FRIENDS OVER FOR A FRIENDLY GAME OF POE-KER. HER FAVORITE OPPONENT WAS EDGAR ALLEN POE. SHE ALMOST ALWAYS WON.
SORRY, ED!

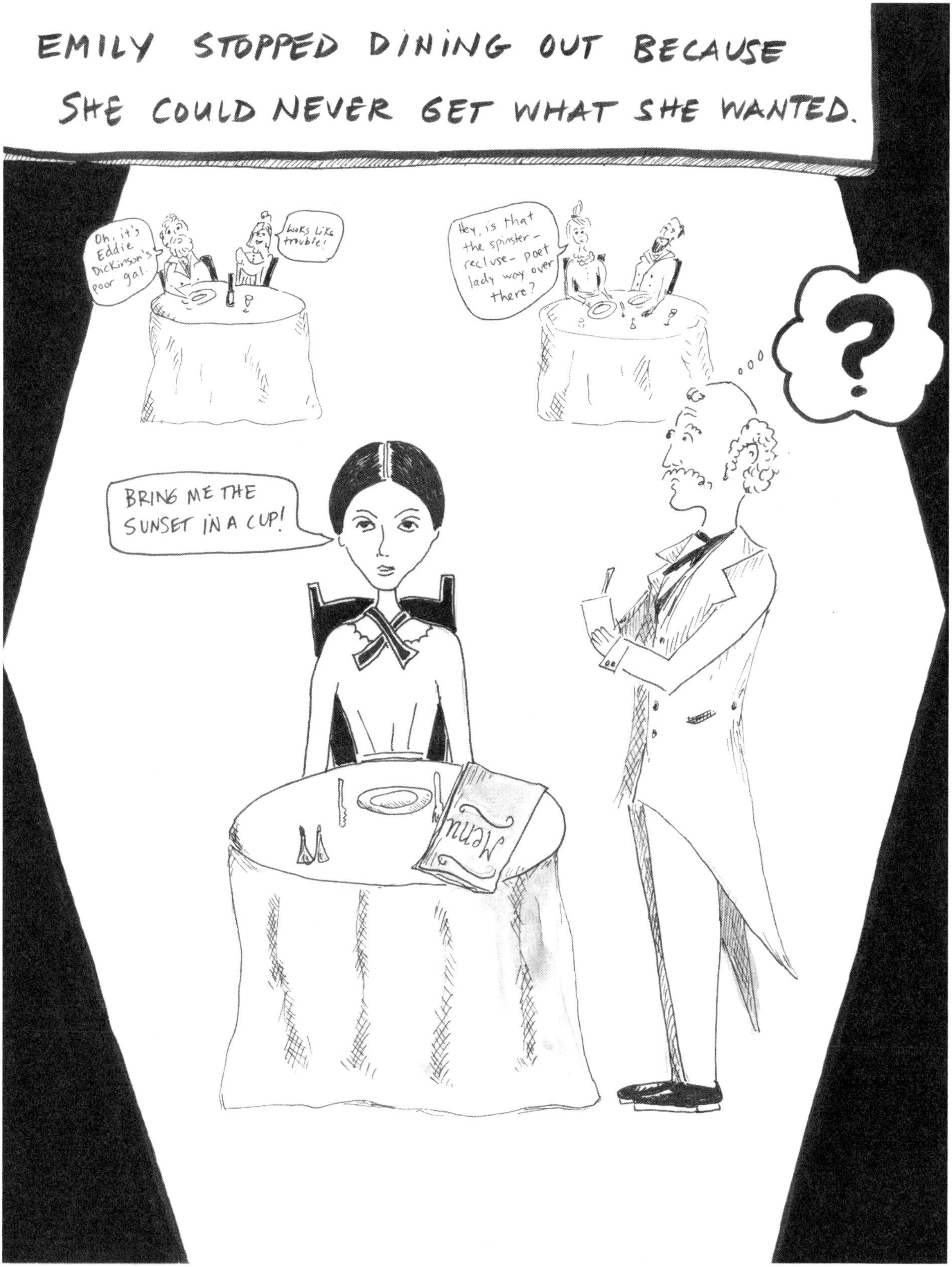
EMILY STOPPED DINING OUT BECAUSE SHE COULD NEVER GET WHAT SHE WANTED.
Oh, it's Eddie Dickinson's poor gal.
Looks like trouble!
Hey, is that the spinster-recluse-poet lady way over there?
?
BRING ME THE SUNSET IN A CUP!
Menu

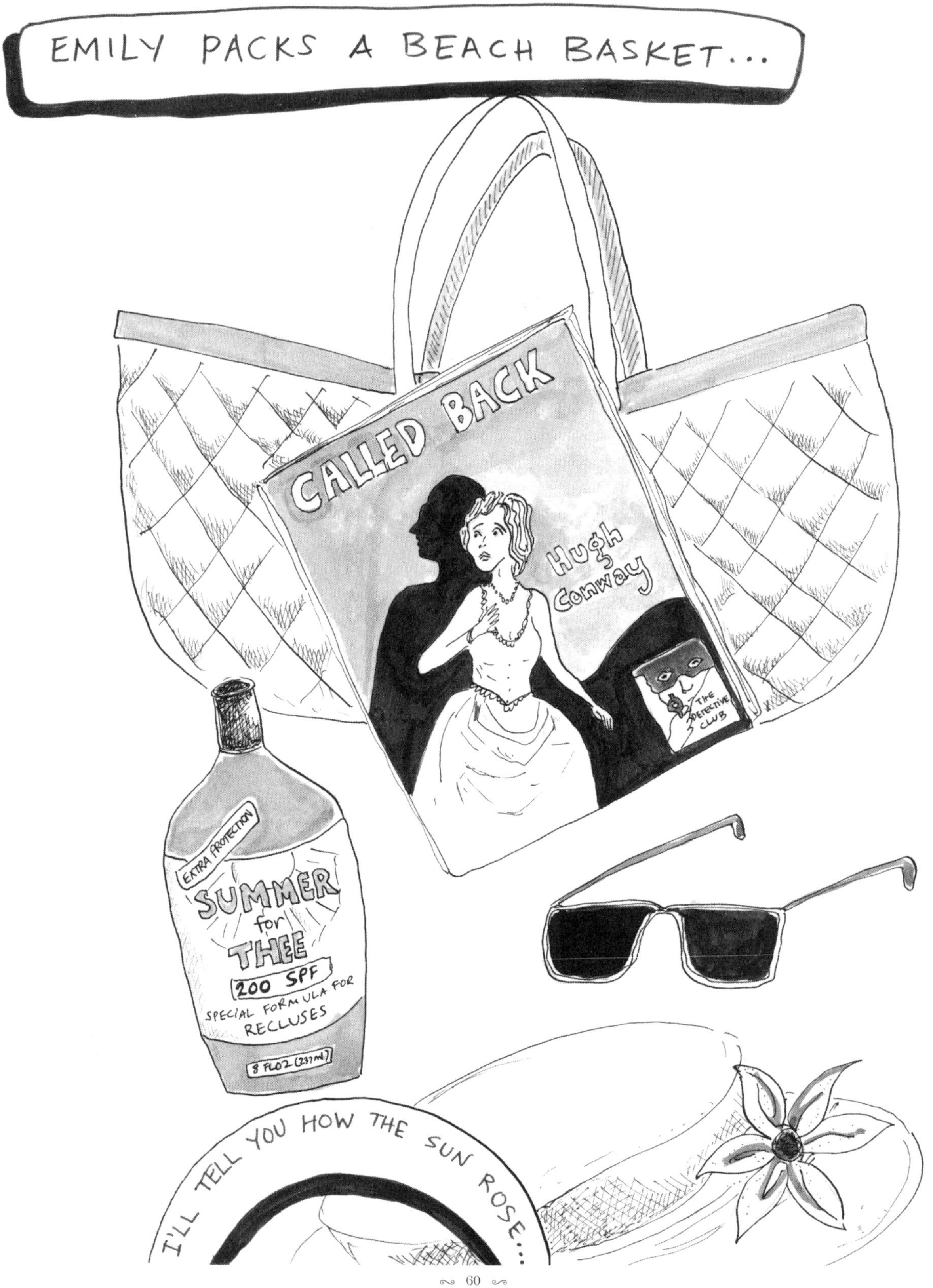
EMILY PACKS A BEACH BASKET...
CALLED BACK
Hugh Conway
THE DETECTIVE CLUB
EXTRA PROTECTION
SUMMER for THEE
200 SPF
SPECIAL FORMULA FOR RECLUSES
8 FL OZ (237 ml)
I'LL TELL YOU HOW THE SUN ROSE...

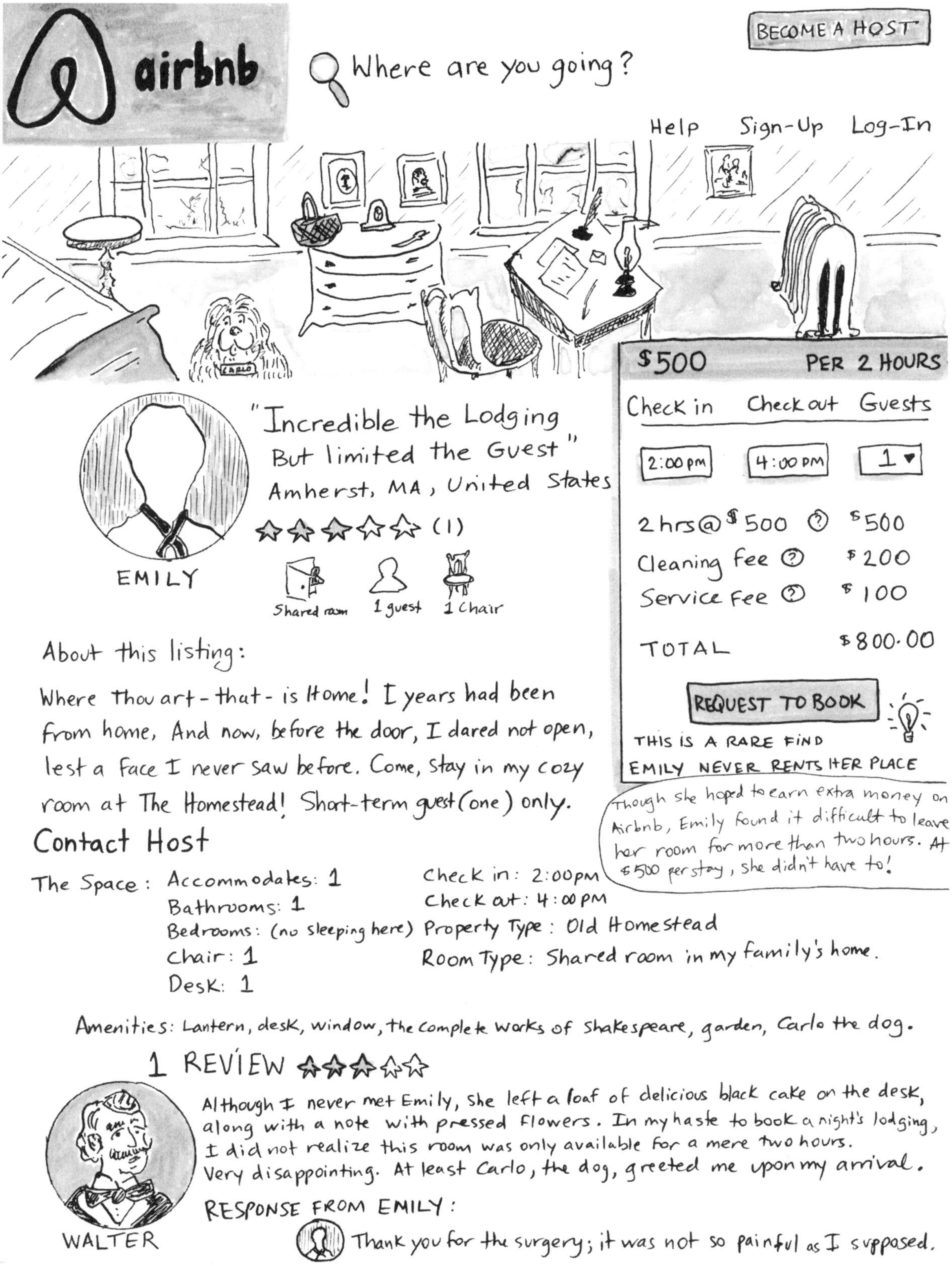
airbnb
Where are you going?
BECOME A HOST
Help
Sign-Up
Log-In
CARLO
$500
PER 2 HOURS
Check in
Check out
Guests
2:00 pm
4:00 PM
1
2 hrs @ $500
$500
Cleaning fee
$200
Service Fee
$100
TOTAL
$800.00
REQUEST TO BOOK
THIS IS A RARE FIND
EMILY NEVER RENTS HER PLACE
"Incredible the Lodging
But limited the Guest"
Amherst, MA, United States
(1)
EMILY
Shared room
1 guest
1 Chair
About this listing:
Where thou art - that - is Home! I years had been from home, And now, before the door, I dared not open, lest a Face I never saw before. Come, stay in my cozy room at The Homestead! Short-term guest (one) only.
Though she hoped to earn extra money on Airbnb, Emily found it difficult to leave her room for more than two hours. At $500 per stay, she didn't have to!
Contact Host
The Space:
Accommodates: 1
Bathrooms: 1
Bedrooms: (no sleeping here)
Chair: 1
Desk: 1
Check in: 2:00pm
Check out: 4:00 PM
Property Type: Old Homestead
Room Type: Shared room in my family's home.
Amenities: Lantern, desk, window, the complete works of Shakespeare, garden, Carlo the dog.
1 REVIEW
Although I never met Emily, she left a loaf of delicious black cake on the desk, along with a note with pressed flowers. In my haste to book a night's lodging, I did not realize this room was only available for a mere two hours. Very disappointing. At least Carlo, the dog, greeted me upon my arrival.
WALTER
RESPONSE FROM EMILY:
Thank you for the surgery; it was not so painful as I supposed.

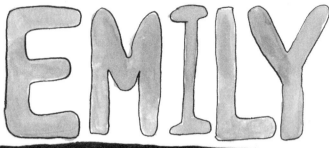

COUNTING THE DAYS WITH EMILY

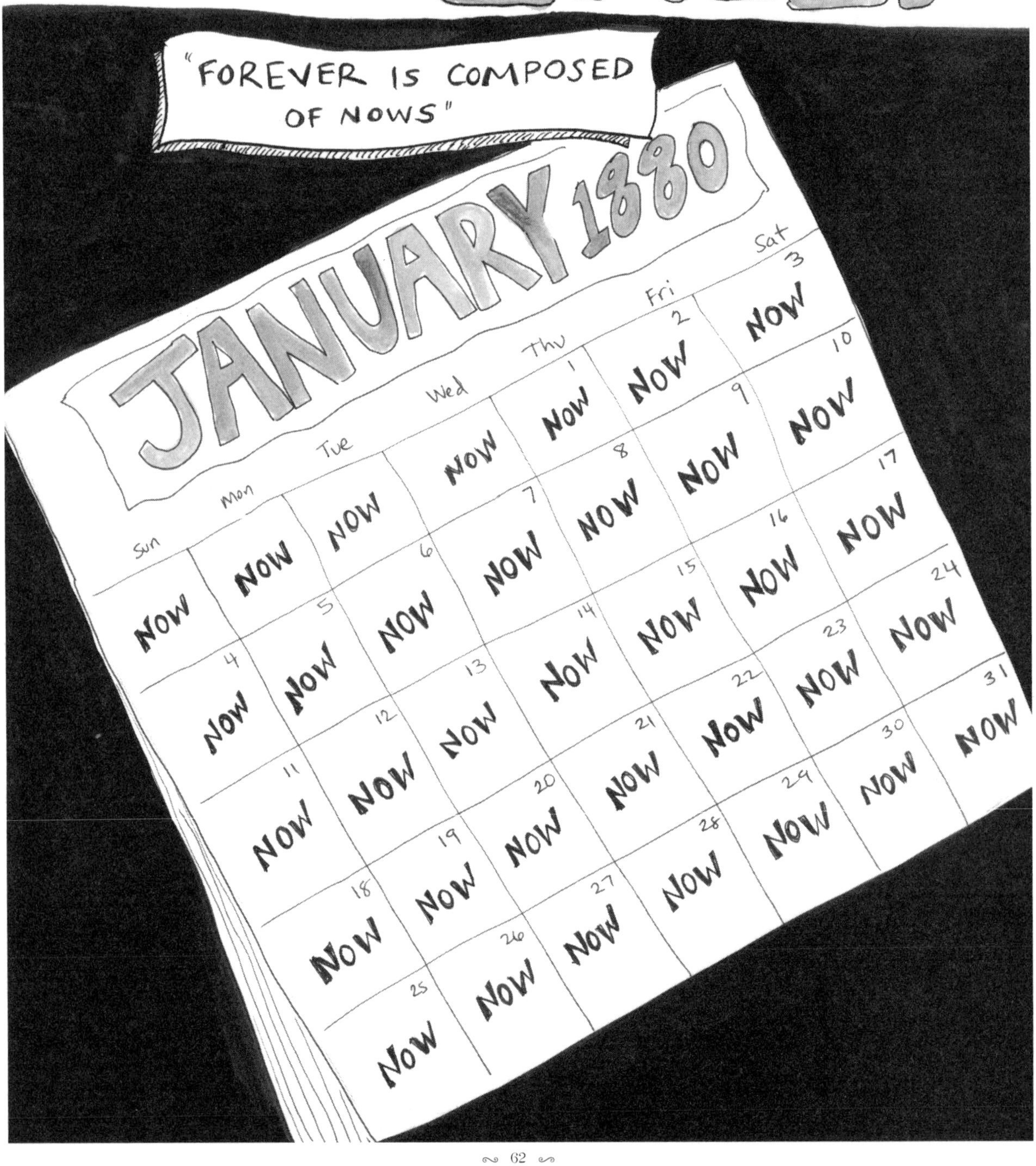
"FOREVER IS COMPOSED OF NOWS"
JANUARY 1880
Sun Mon Tue Wed Thu Fri Sat
NOW NOW NOW NOW 1 NOW 2 NOW 3 NOW
4 NOW 5 NOW 6 NOW 7 NOW 8 NOW 9 NOW 10 NOW
11 NOW 12 NOW 13 NOW 14 NOW 15 NOW 16 NOW 17 NOW
18 NOW 19 NOW 20 NOW 21 NOW 22 NOW 23 NOW 24 NOW
25 NOW 26 NOW 27 NOW 28 NOW 29 NOW 30 NOW 31 NOW

DICKINSON

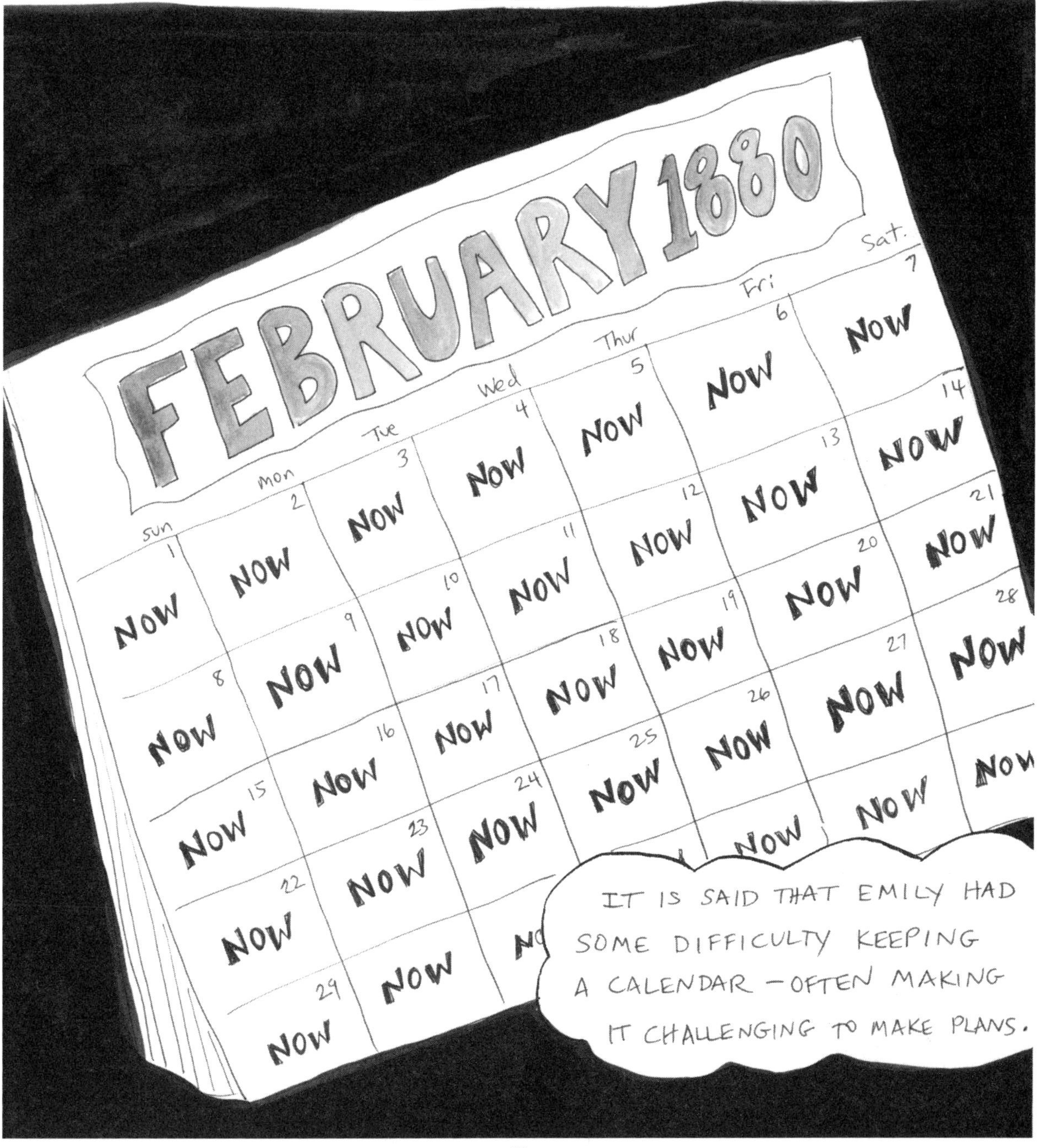
FEBRUARY 1880
Sun Mon Tue Wed Thur Fri Sat.
IT IS SAID THAT EMILY HAD SOME DIFFICULTY KEEPING A CALENDAR — OFTEN MAKING IT CHALLENGING TO MAKE PLANS.

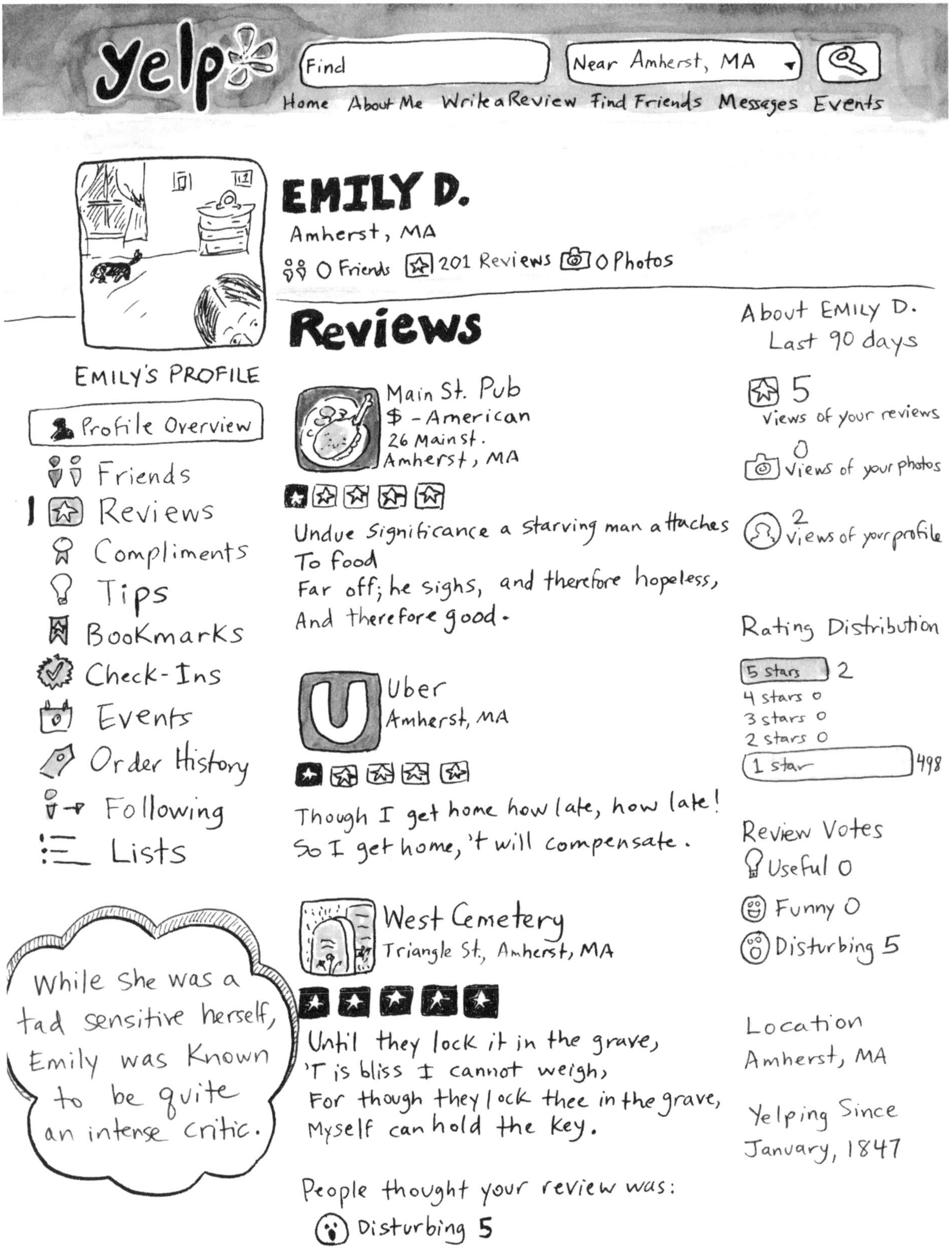

yelp

Find | Near Amherst, MA ▾ | 🔍

Home   About Me   Write a Review   Find Friends   Messages   Events

EMILY D.

Amherst, MA

👥 0 Friends   ⭐ 201 Reviews   📷 0 Photos

EMILY'S PROFILE

👤 Profile Overview

👥 Friends

| ⭐ Reviews

🎗 Compliments

💡 Tips

🔖 Bookmarks

✅ Check-Ins

📅 Events

🖊 Order History

👣 Following

☰ Lists

> While she was a tad sensitive herself, Emily was known to be quite an intense critic.

Reviews

  Main St. Pub
$ – American
26 Main st.
Amherst, MA

★★★★★

Undue Significance a starving man attaches
To food
Far off; he sighs, and therefore hopeless,
And therefore good.

U Uber
Amherst, MA

★★★★★

Though I get home how late, how late!
So I get home, 't will compensate.

  West Cemetery
Triangle St., Amherst, MA

★★★★★

Until they lock it in the grave,
'T is bliss I cannot weigh,
For though they lock thee in the grave,
Myself can hold the key.

People thought your review was:
😮 Disturbing 5

About EMILY D.
Last 90 days

⭐ **5**
Views of your reviews

📷 0
Views of your photos

👤 2
Views of your profile

Rating Distribution

5 stars	2
4 stars	0
3 stars	0
2 stars	0
1 star	498

Review Votes
💡 Useful 0
😊 Funny 0
😮 Disturbing 5

Location
Amherst, MA

Yelping Since
January, 1847

Nature

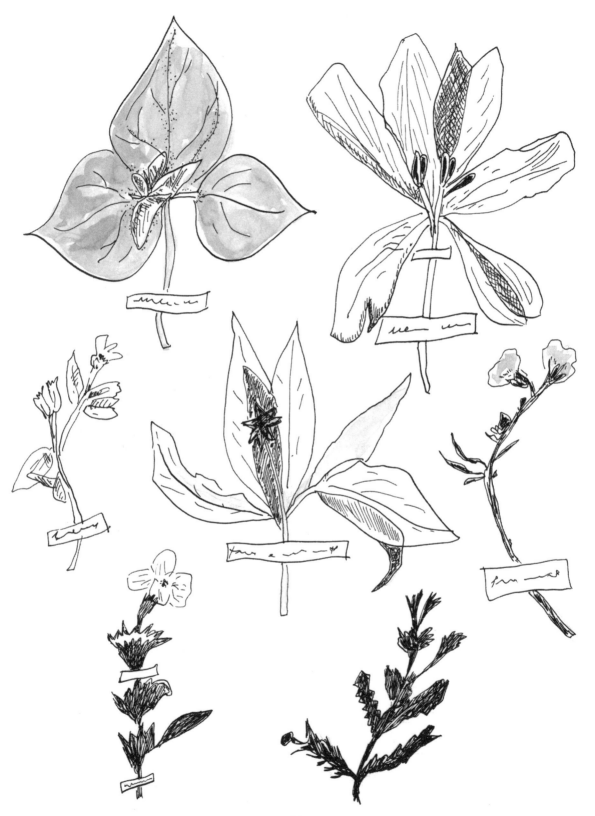

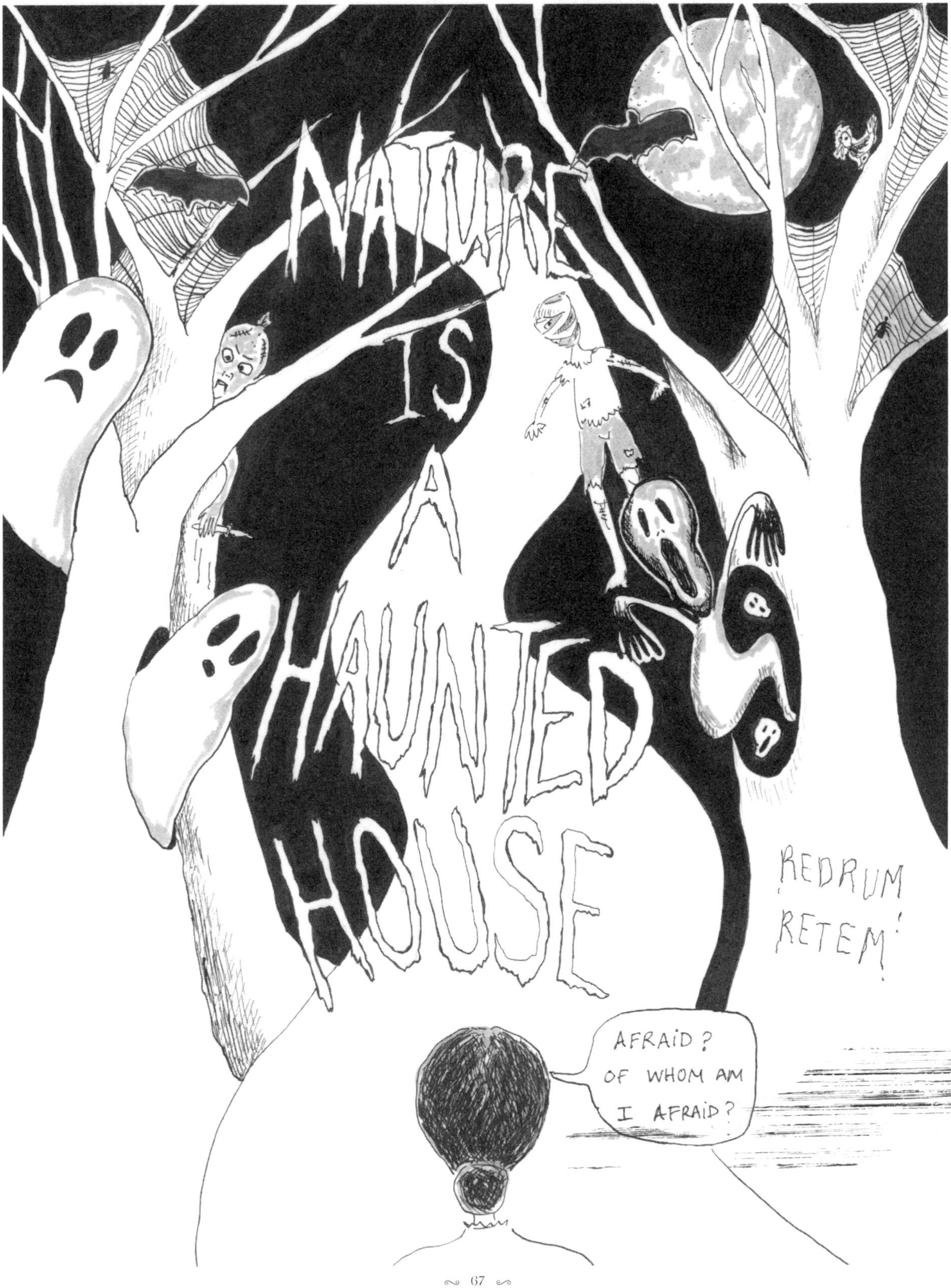
NATURE IS A HAUNTED HOUSE
REDRUM RETEM!
AFRAID? OF WHOM AM I AFRAID?

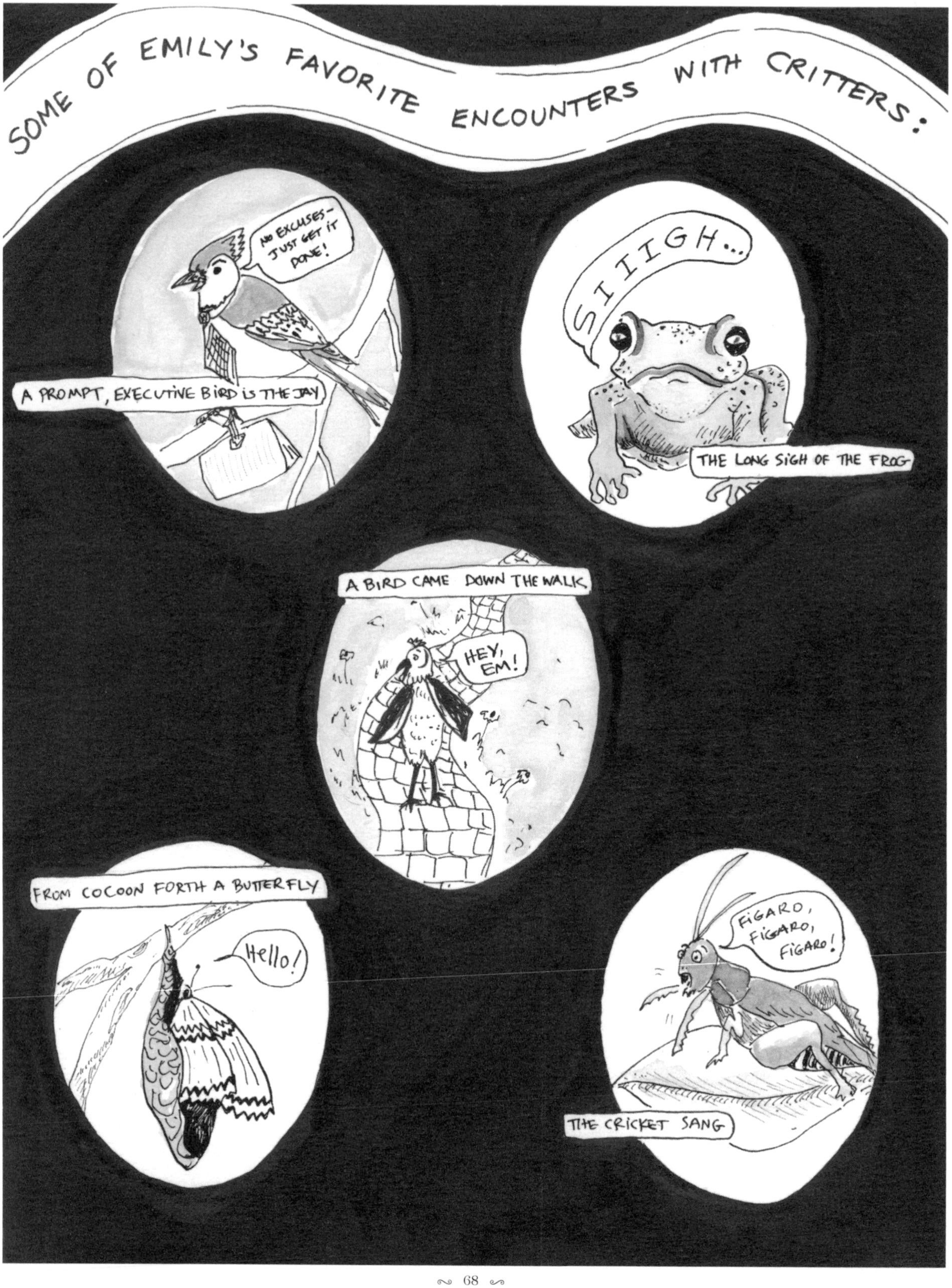
SOME OF EMILY'S FAVORITE ENCOUNTERS WITH CRITTERS:
NO EXCUSES- JUST GET IT DONE!
A PROMPT, EXECUTIVE BIRD IS THE JAY
SIIIGH...
THE LONG SIGH OF THE FROG
A BIRD CAME DOWN THE WALK
HEY, EM!
FROM COCOON FORTH A BUTTERFLY
Hello!
FIGARO, FIGARO, FIGARO!
THE CRICKET SANG

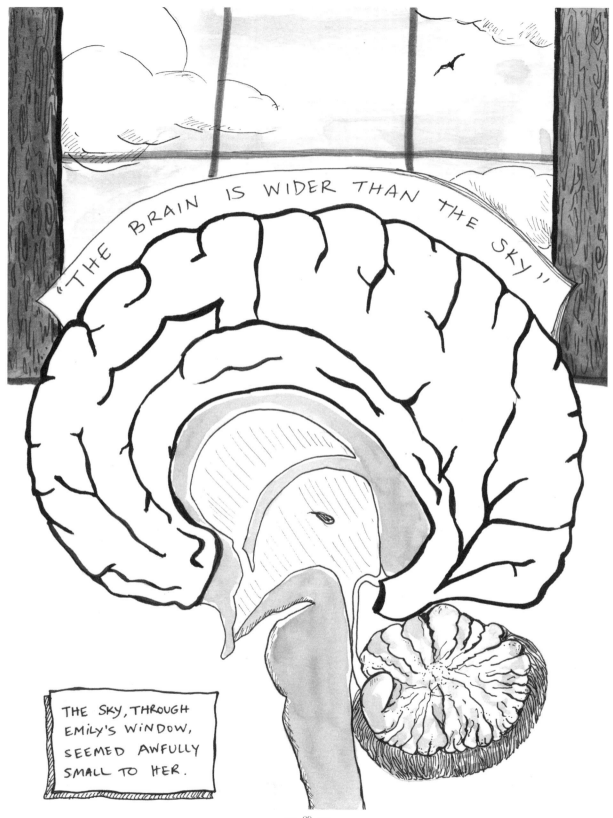

"THE BRAIN IS WIDER THAN THE SKY"

THE SKY, THROUGH EMILY'S WINDOW, SEEMED AWFULLY SMALL TO HER.

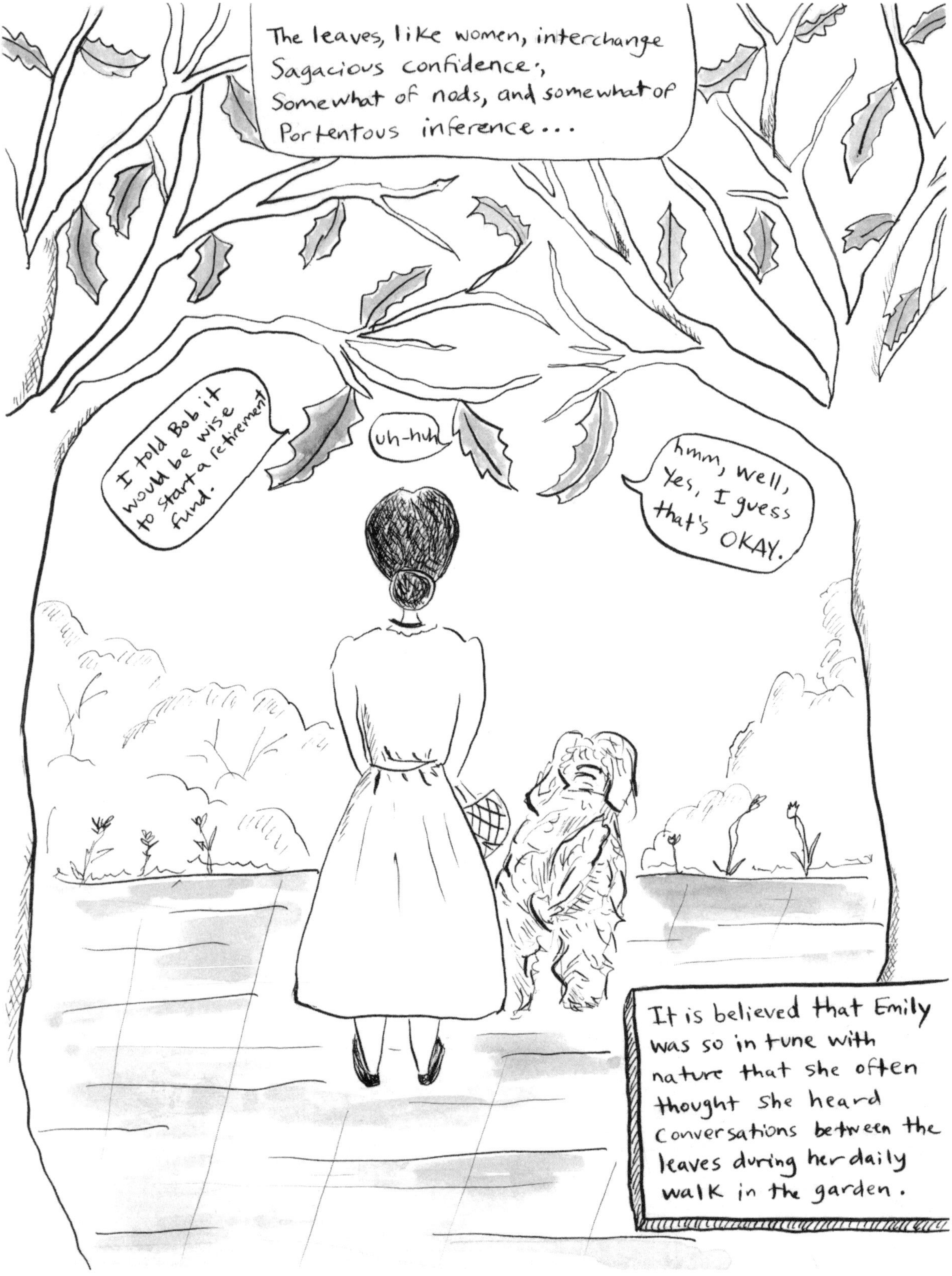
The leaves, like women, interchange
Sagacious confidence;
Somewhat of nods, and somewhat of
Portentous inference...
I told Bob it would be wise to start a retirement fund.
uh-huh
hmm, well, Yes, I guess that's OKAY.
It is believed that Emily was so in tune with nature that she often thought she heard conversations between the leaves during her daily walk in the garden.

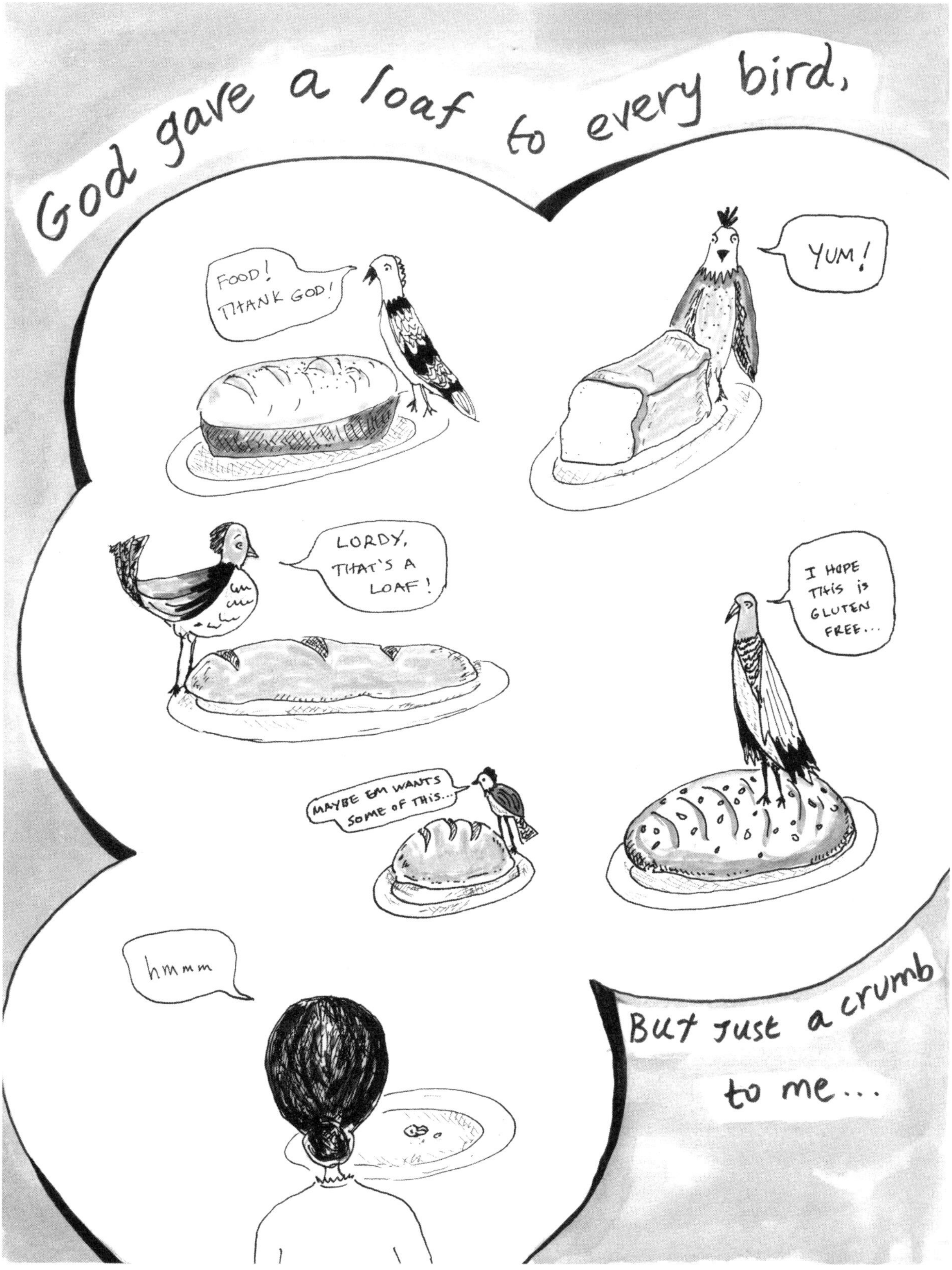
God gave a loaf to every bird,
FOOD! THANK GOD!
YUM!
LORDY, THAT'S A LOAF!
I HOPE THIS IS GLUTEN FREE...
MAYBE EM WANTS SOME OF THIS...
hmmm
But just a crumb to me...

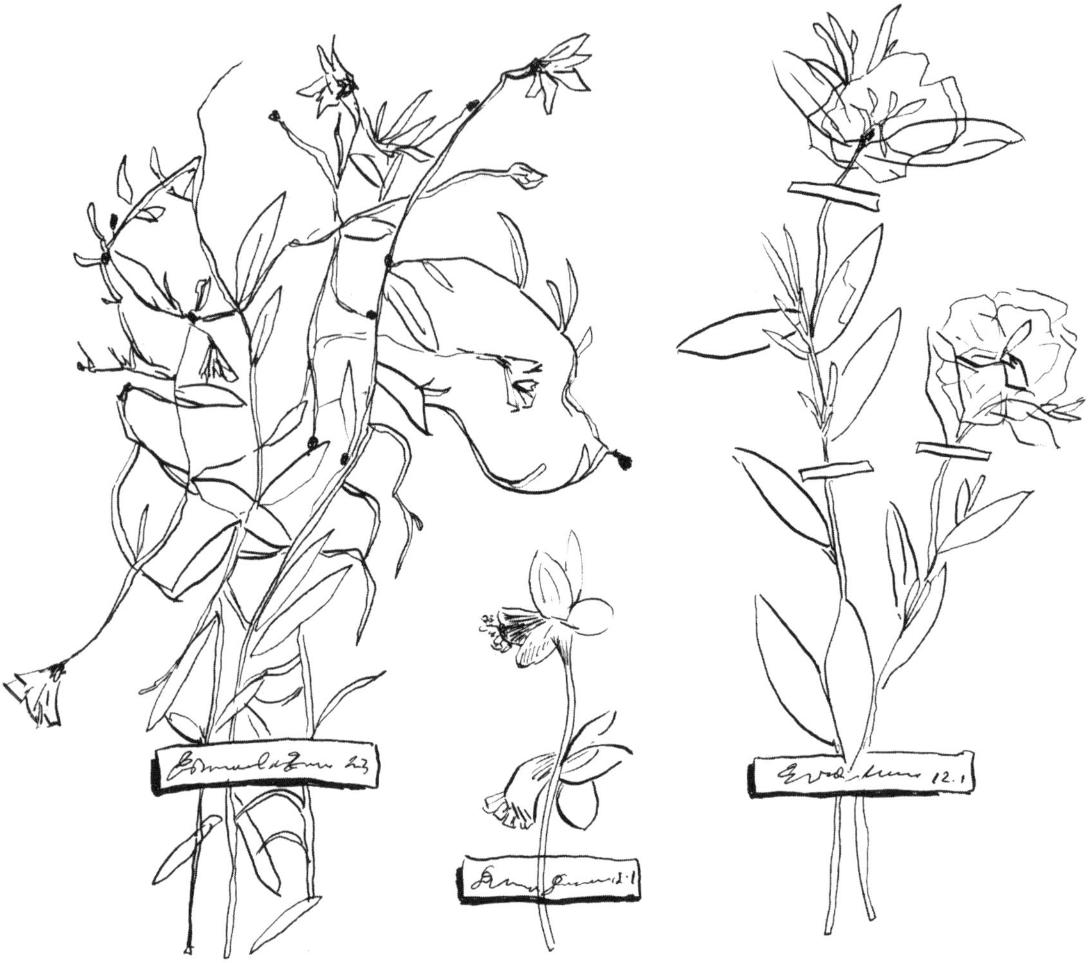

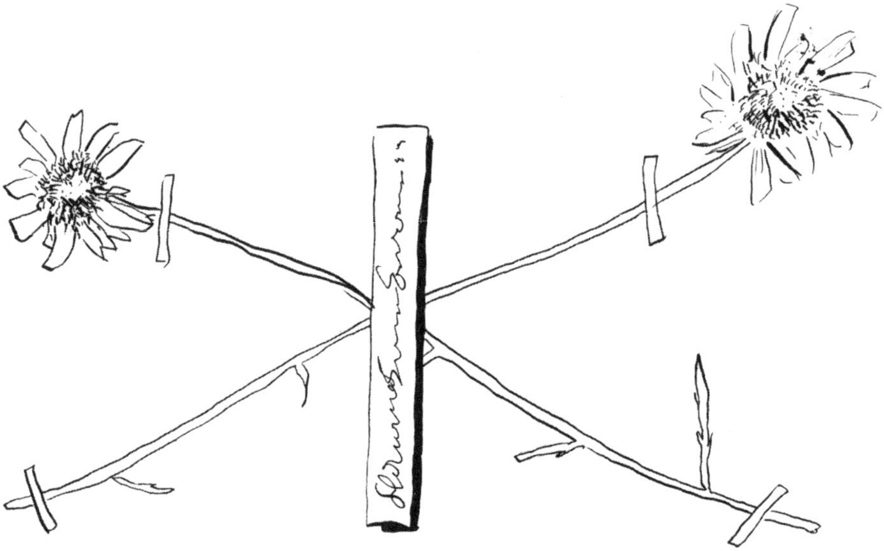

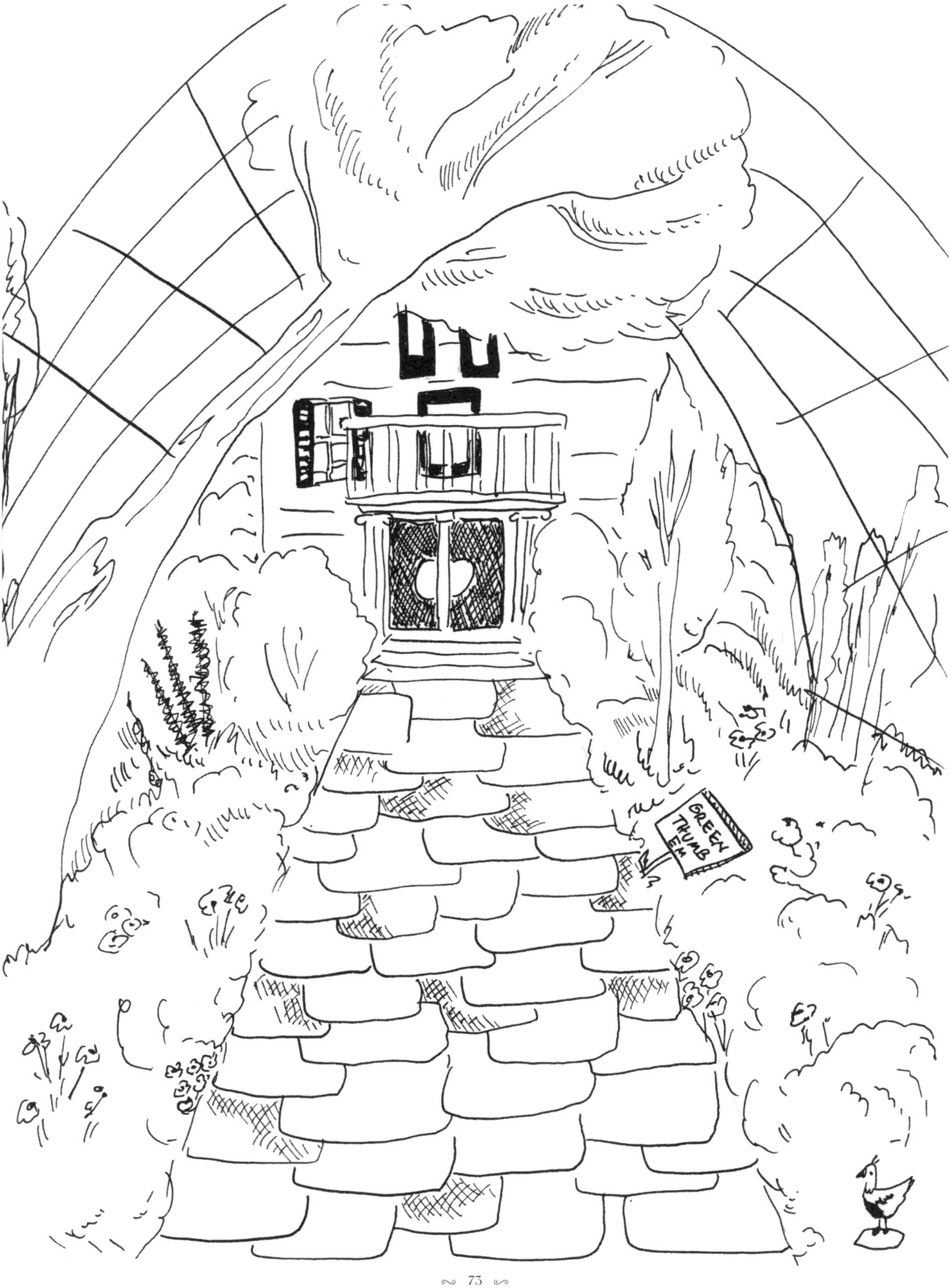
GREEN THUMB EM

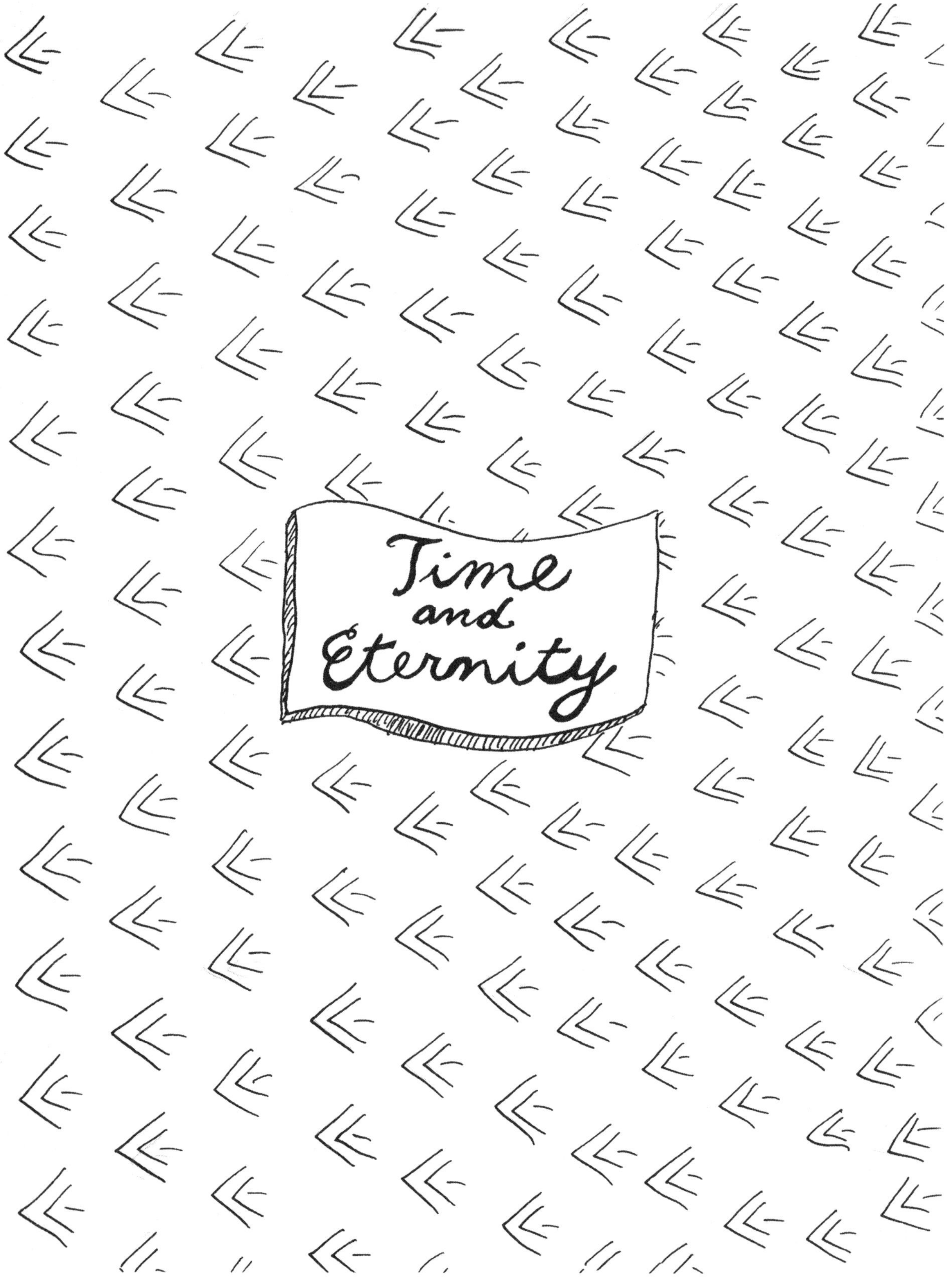
Time and Eternity

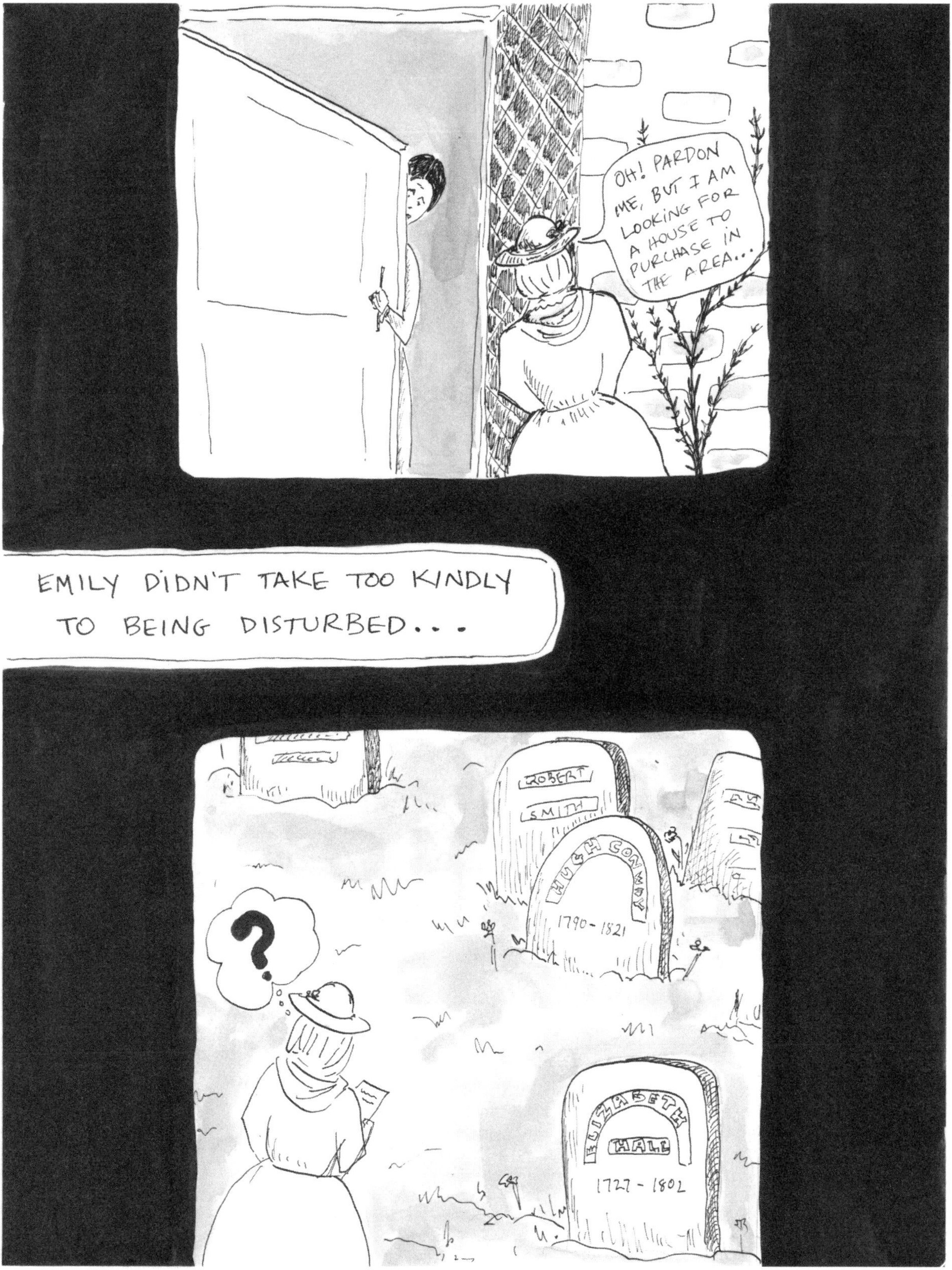
OH! PARDON ME, BUT I AM LOOKING FOR A HOUSE TO PURCHASE IN THE AREA...
EMILY DIDN'T TAKE TOO KINDLY TO BEING DISTURBED...
ROBERT
SMITH
HUGH CONWAY
1790 - 1821
?
ELIZABETH
HALE
1727 - 1802

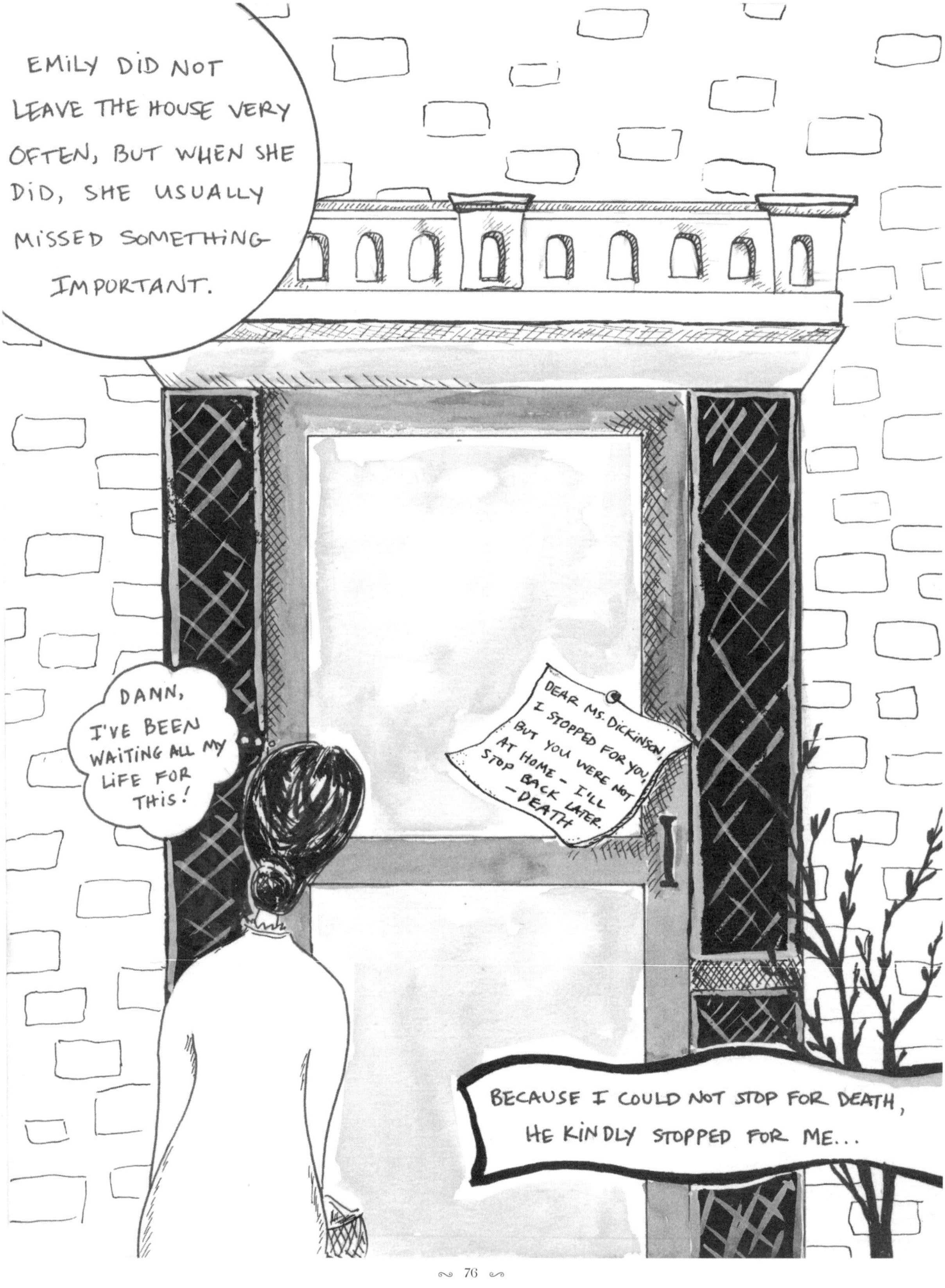
EMILY DID NOT LEAVE THE HOUSE VERY OFTEN, BUT WHEN SHE DID, SHE USUALLY MISSED SOMETHING IMPORTANT.
DANN, I'VE BEEN WAITING ALL MY LIFE FOR THIS!
DEAR MS. DICKINSON, I STOPPED FOR YOU, BUT YOU WERE NOT AT HOME - I'LL STOP BACK LATER. -DEATH
BECAUSE I COULD NOT STOP FOR DEATH, HE KINDLY STOPPED FOR ME...

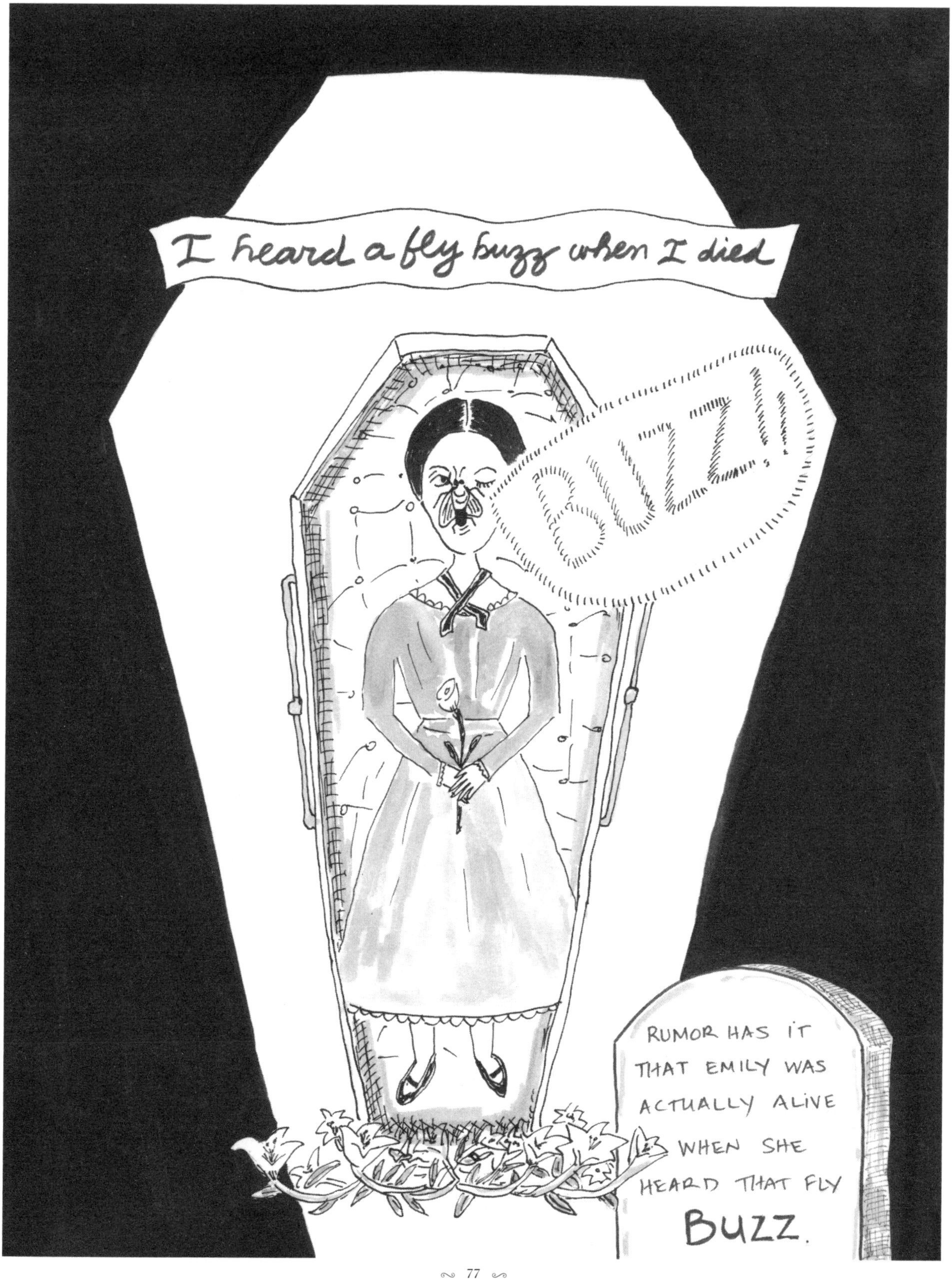
I heard a fly buzz when I died
BUZZ!!
RUMOR HAS IT THAT EMILY WAS ACTUALLY ALIVE WHEN SHE HEARD THAT FLY BUZZ.

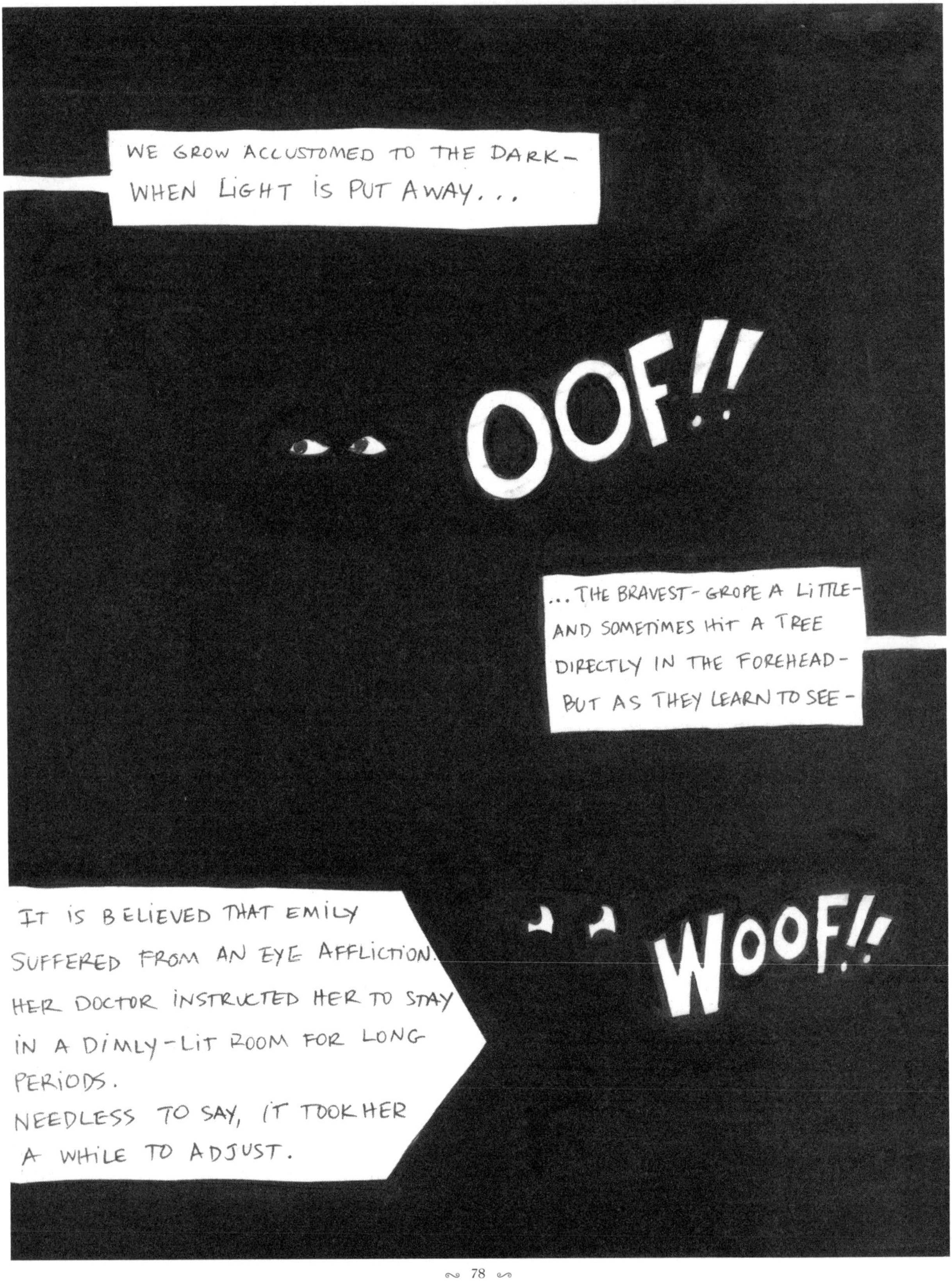
WE GROW ACCUSTOMED TO THE DARK-
WHEN LIGHT IS PUT AWAY...
OOF!!
...THE BRAVEST- GROPE A LITTLE- AND SOMETIMES HIT A TREE DIRECTLY IN THE FOREHEAD- BUT AS THEY LEARN TO SEE-
IT IS BELIEVED THAT EMILY SUFFERED FROM AN EYE AFFLICTION. HER DOCTOR INSTRUCTED HER TO STAY IN A DIMLY-LIT ROOM FOR LONG PERIODS.
NEEDLESS TO SAY, IT TOOK HER A WHILE TO ADJUST.
WOOF!!

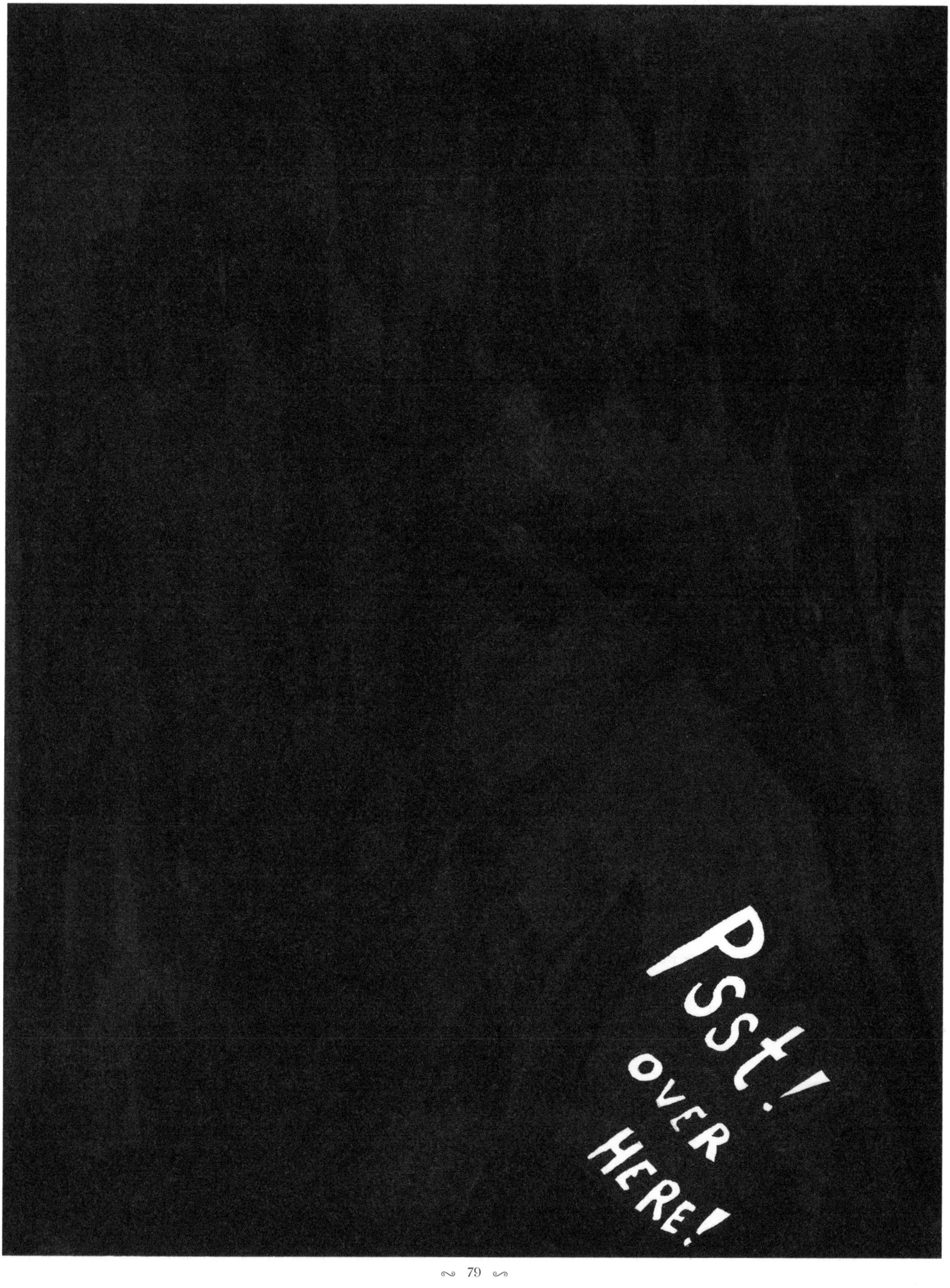
Psst!
OVER
HERE!

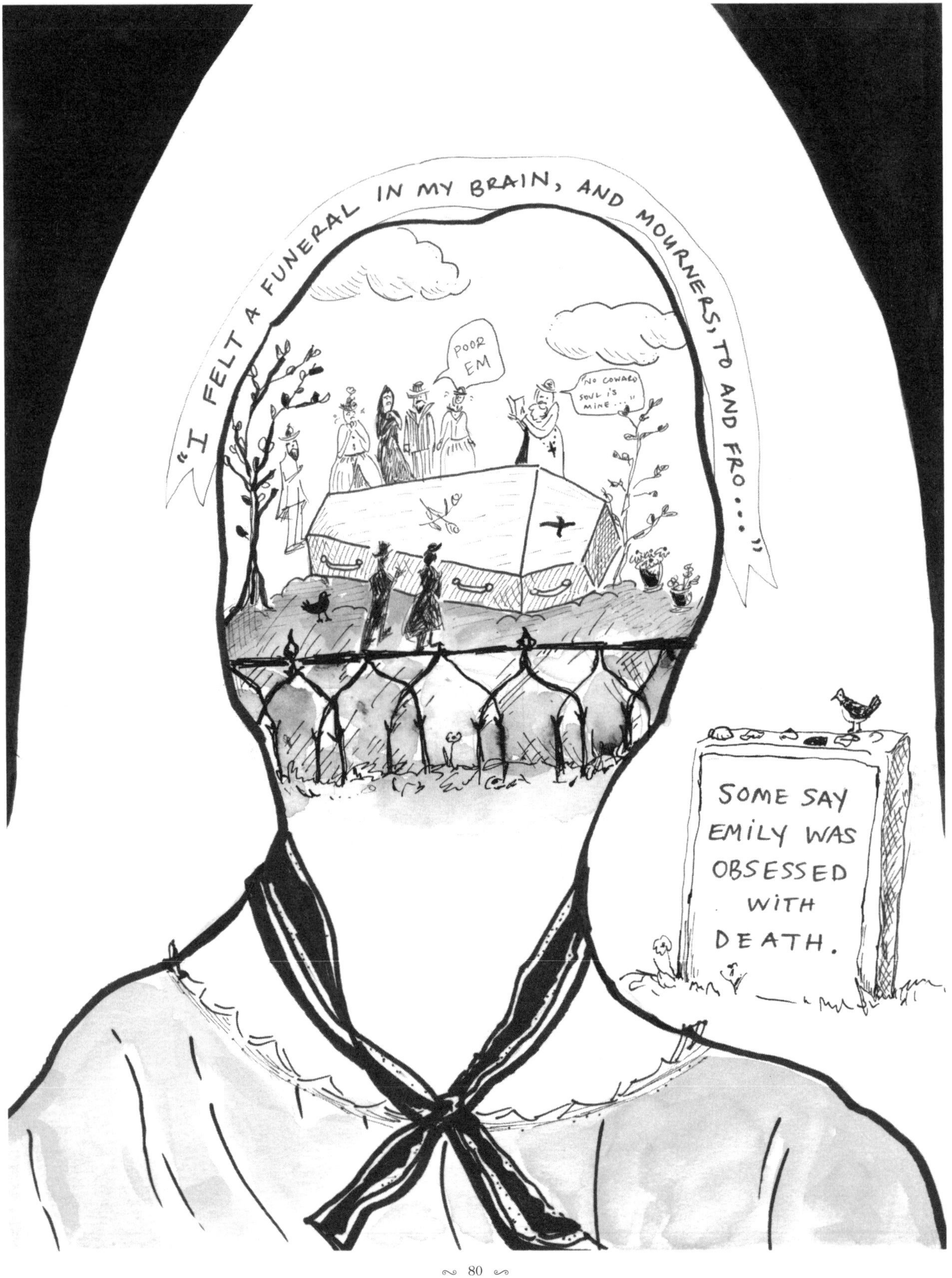
"I FELT A FUNERAL IN MY BRAIN, AND MOURNERS, TO AND FRO..."
POOR EM
"NO COWARD SOUL IS MINE..."
SOME SAY EMILY WAS OBSESSED WITH DEATH.

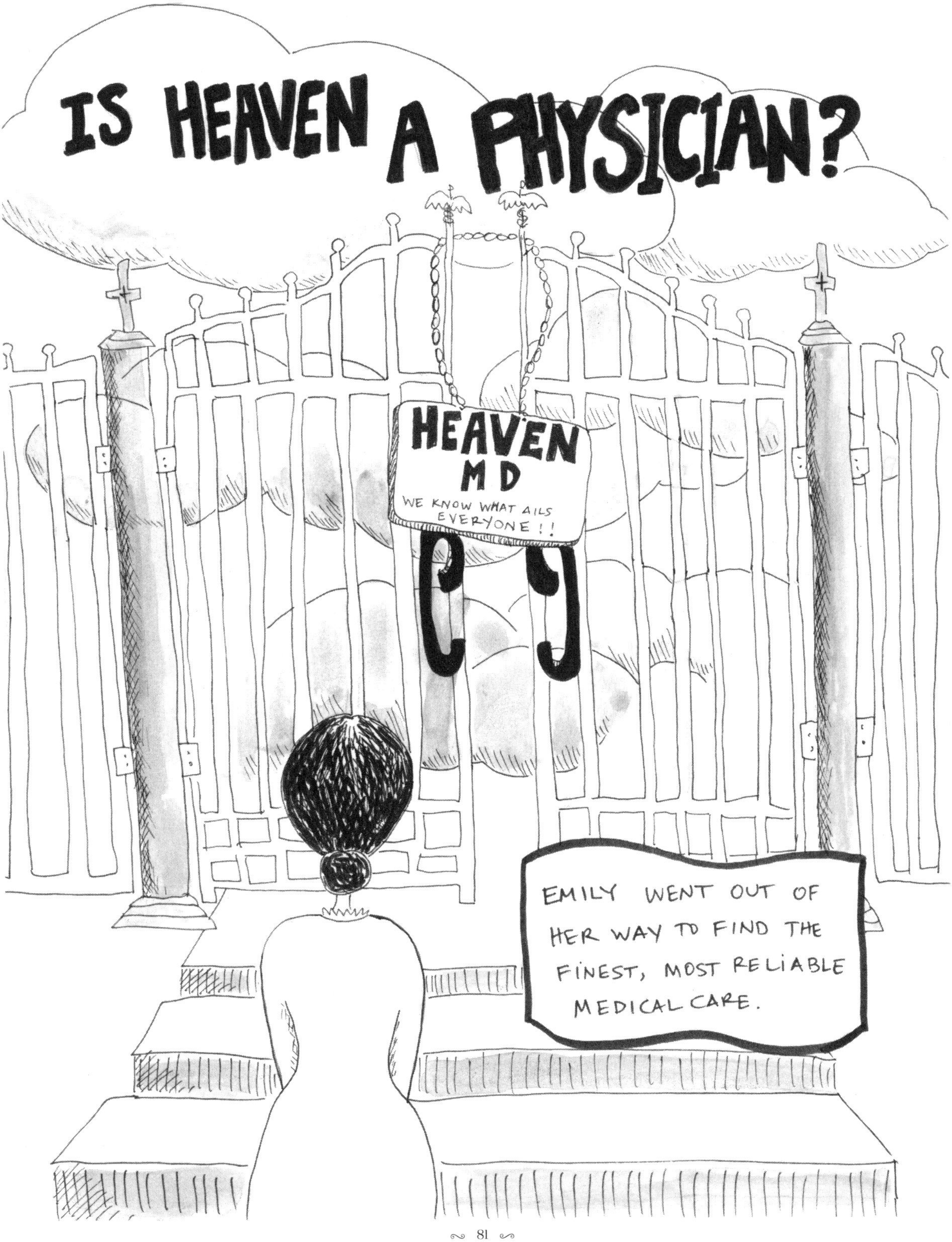

IS HEAVEN A PHYSICIAN?
HEAVEN MD
WE KNOW WHAT AILS EVERYONE!!
EMILY WENT OUT OF HER WAY TO FIND THE FINEST, MOST RELIABLE MEDICAL CARE.

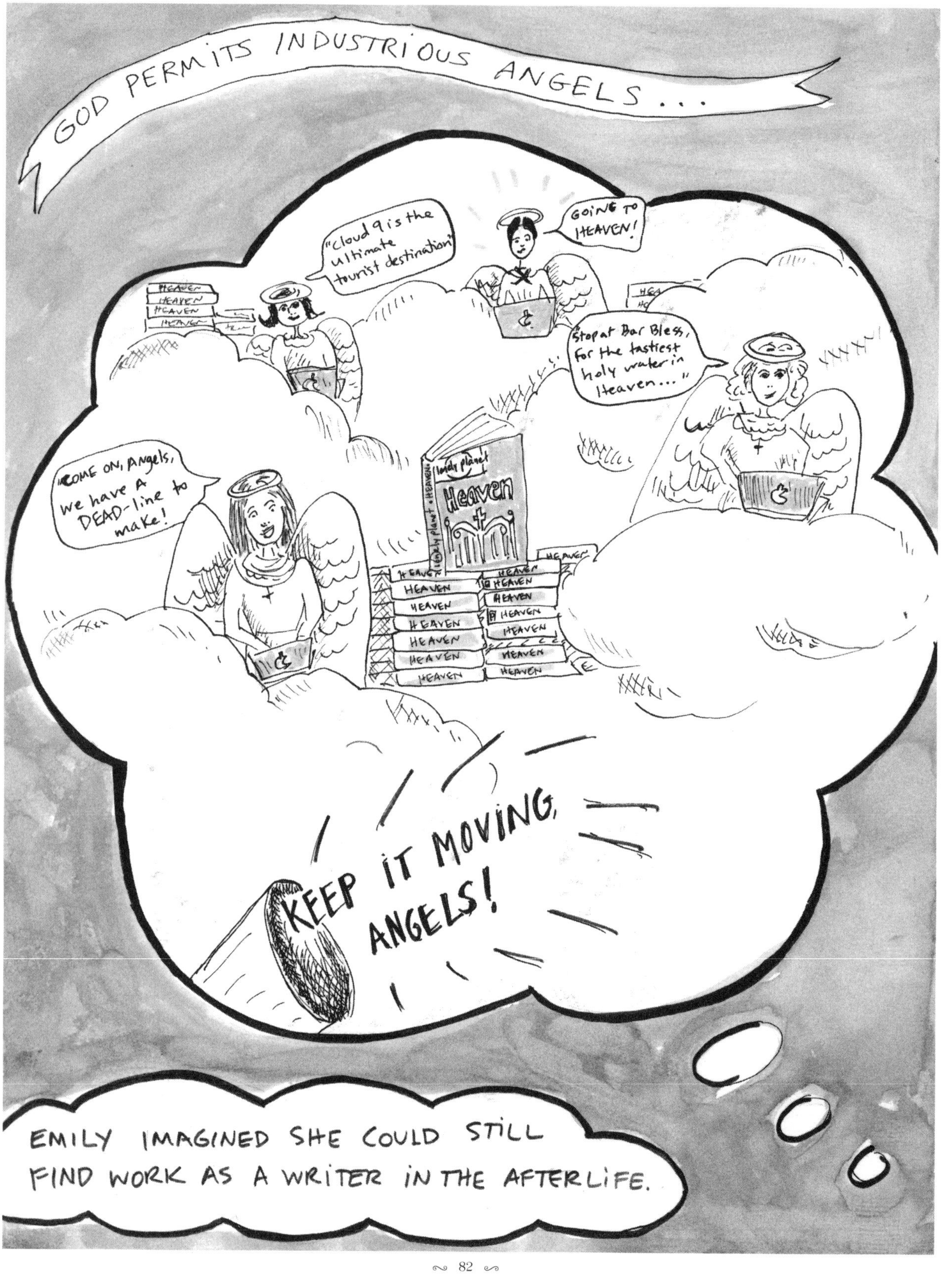
GOD PERMITS INDUSTRIOUS ANGELS...
"Cloud 9 is the ultimate tourist destination"
GOING TO HEAVEN!
"Stop at Bar Bless, for the tastiest holy water in Heaven..."
"COME ON, Angels, we have A DEAD-line to make!
lonely planet HEAVEN
Heaven
HEAVEN
KEEP IT MOVING, ANGELS!
EMILY IMAGINED SHE COULD STILL FIND WORK AS A WRITER IN THE AFTERLIFE.

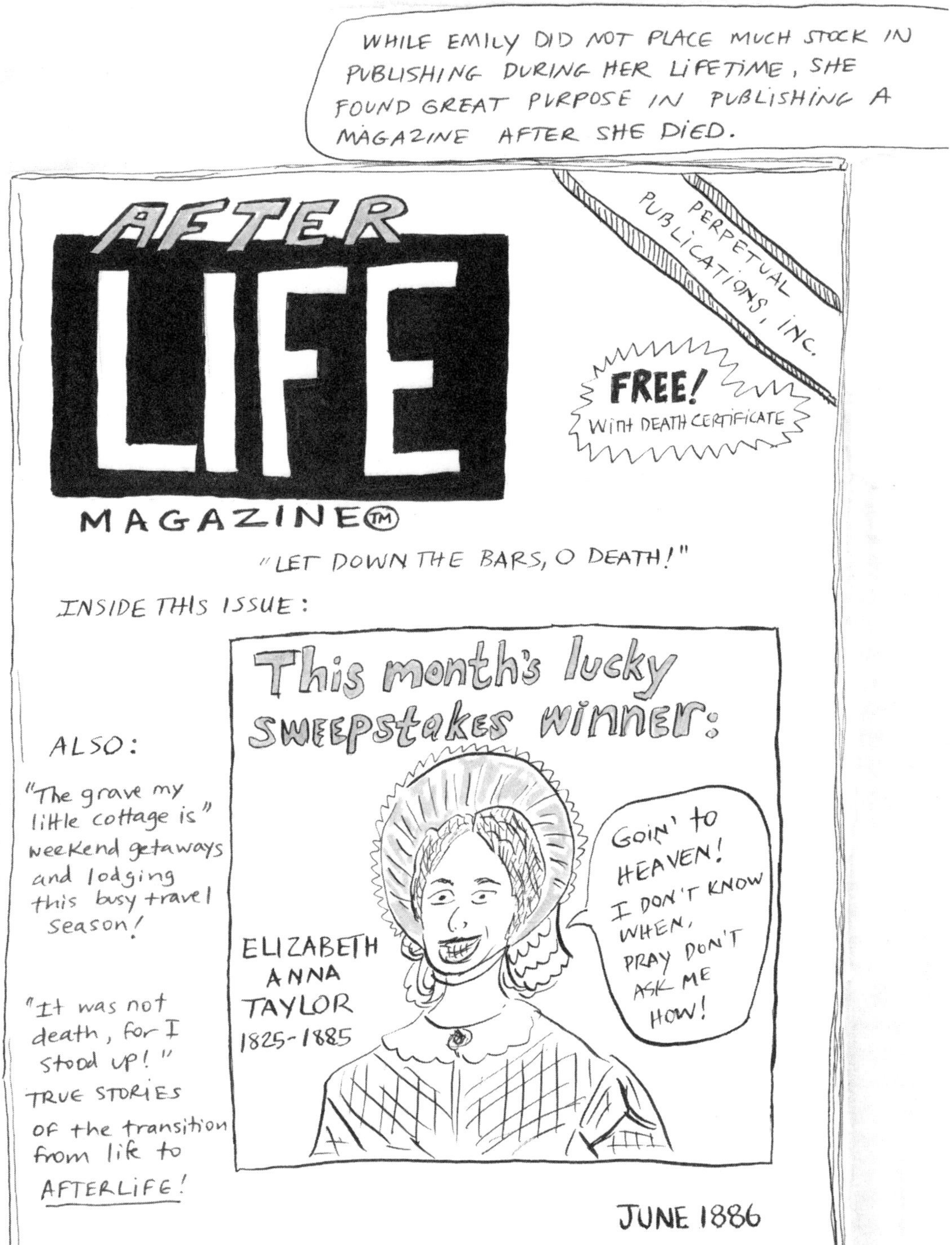

WHILE EMILY DID NOT PLACE MUCH STOCK IN PUBLISHING DURING HER LIFETIME, SHE FOUND GREAT PURPOSE IN PUBLISHING A MAGAZINE AFTER SHE DIED.
AFTER LIFE
MAGAZINE™
PERPETUAL PUBLICATIONS, INC.
FREE! WITH DEATH CERTIFICATE
"LET DOWN THE BARS, O DEATH!"
INSIDE THIS ISSUE:
This month's lucky sweepstakes winner:
ELIZABETH ANNA TAYLOR 1825-1885
Goin' to HEAVEN! I DON'T KNOW WHEN, PRAY DON'T ASK ME HOW!
ALSO:
"The grave my little cottage is" weekend getaways and lodging this busy travel season!
"It was not death, for I stood up!" TRUE STORIES of the transition from life to AFTERLIFE!
JUNE 1886

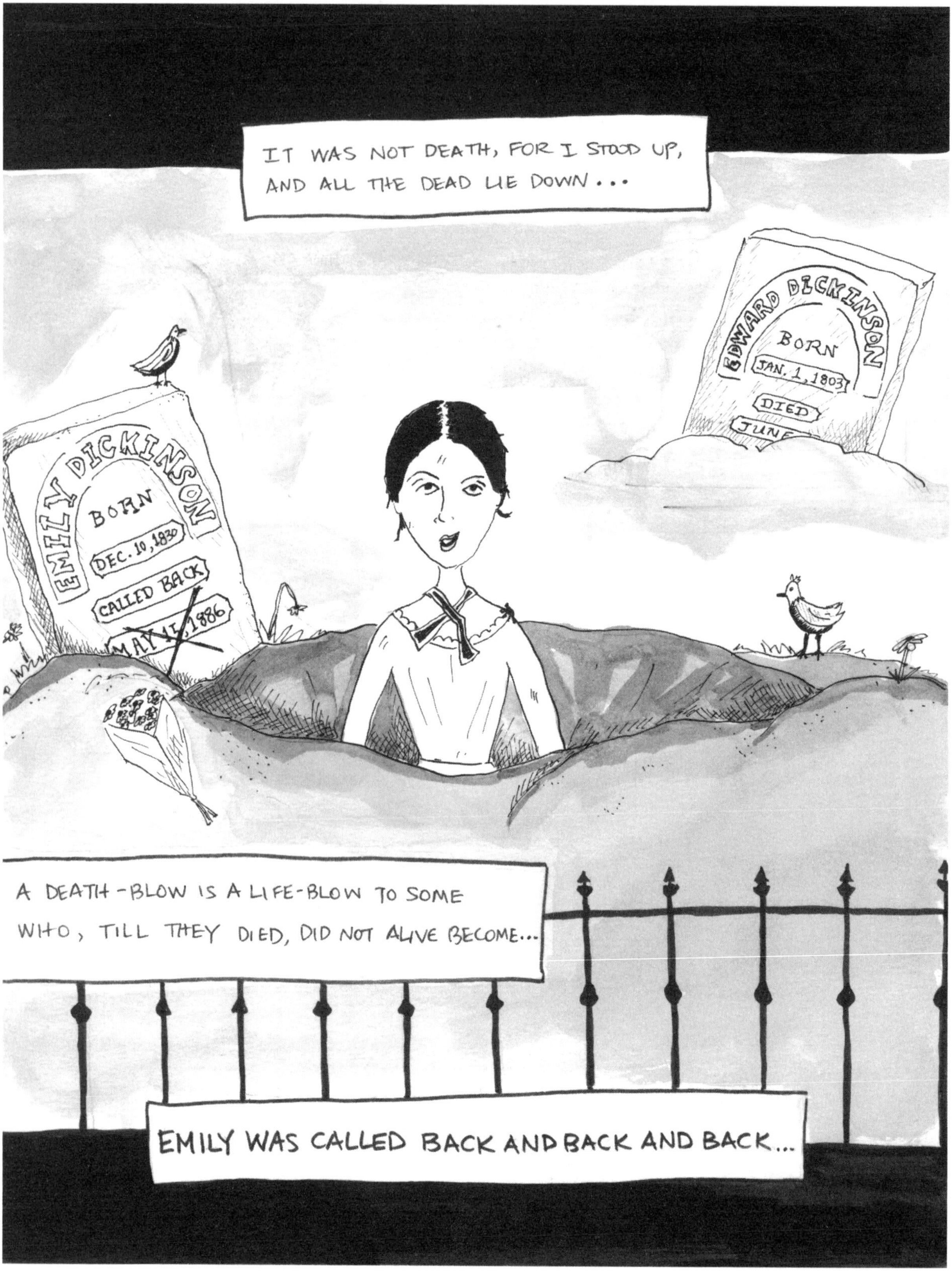
IT WAS NOT DEATH, FOR I STOOD UP, AND ALL THE DEAD LIE DOWN...
EDWARD DICKINSON BORN JAN. 1, 1803 DIED JUNE
EMILY DICKINSON BORN DEC. 10, 1830 CALLED BACK MAY 15, 1886
A DEATH-BLOW IS A LIFE-BLOW TO SOME WHO, TILL THEY DIED, DID NOT ALIVE BECOME...
EMILY WAS CALLED BACK AND BACK AND BACK...

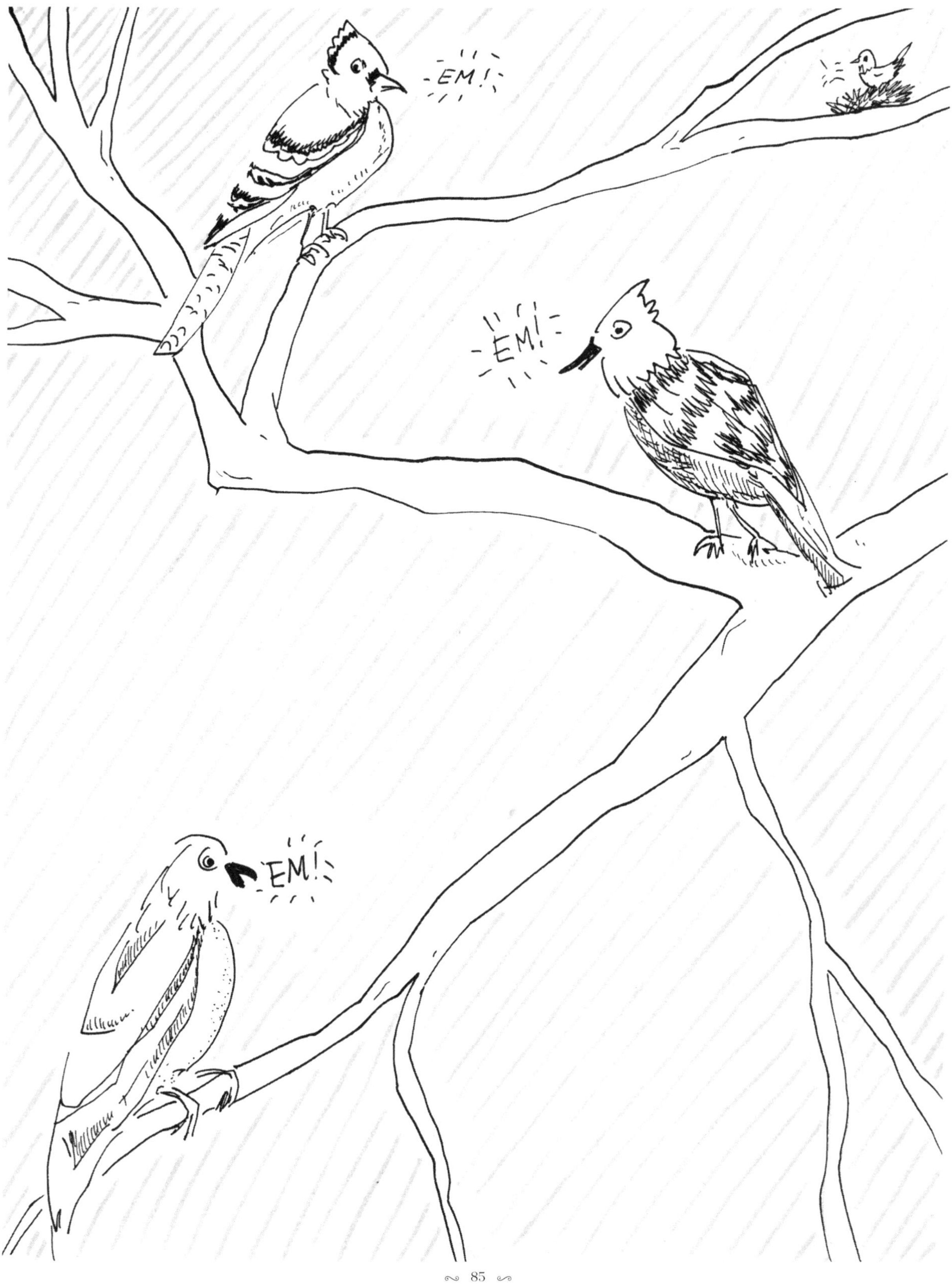
EM!
EM!
EM!

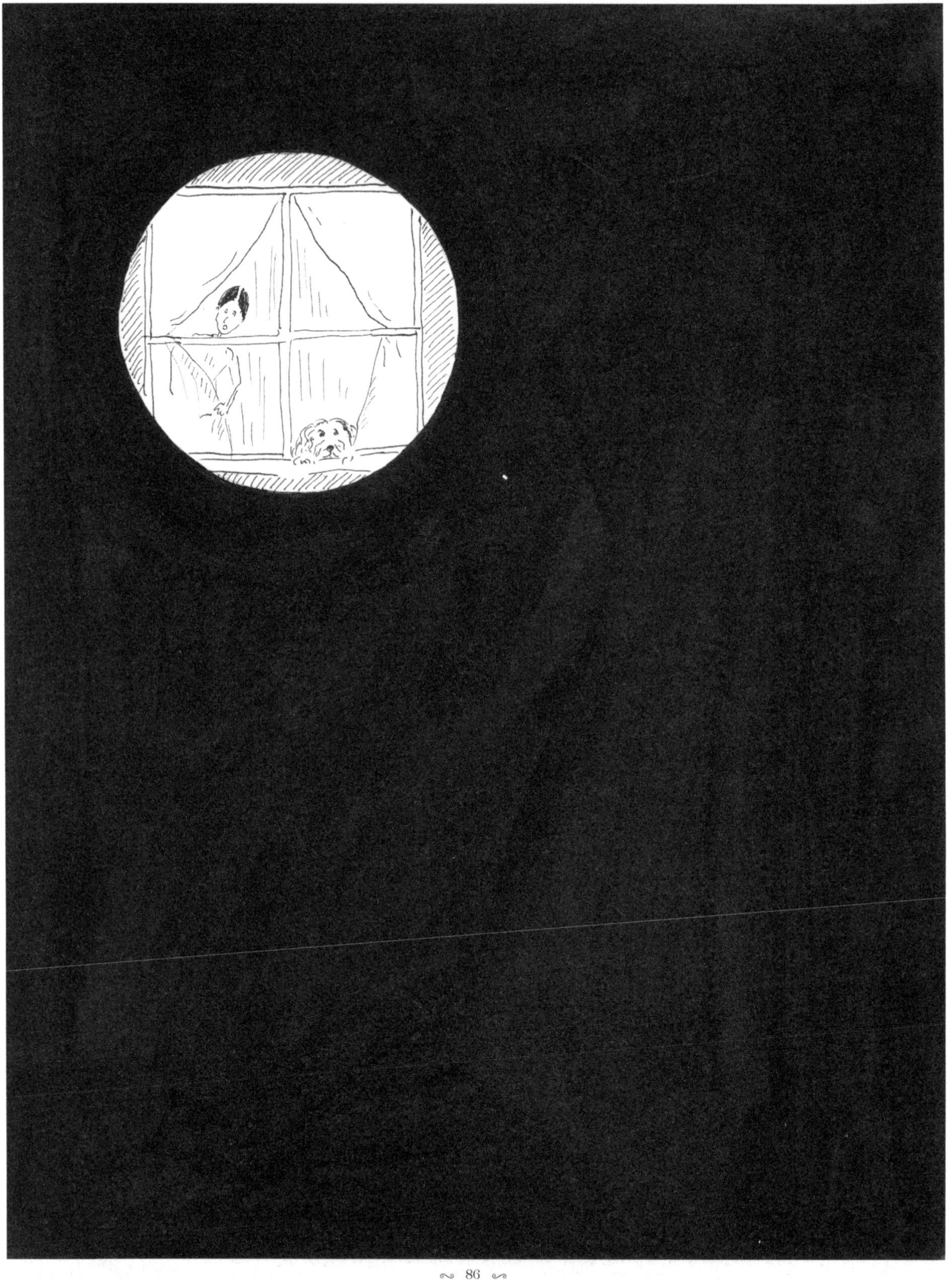

MANY thanks:

To The Corporation of YADDO (a.k.a. Paradise), where this book began. Special thanks to Elaina Richardson, Candace Wait, and to the magnificent Tower room.

To the poets— Cleopatra Mathis, Marianne Boruch, and Jane Hirshfield for their insight into the poems and for their humor.

To the amazing Alison Bechdel for kindly taking a look at this book and for giving such thoughtful comments (for free!), and for putting such inspiring work out there. Thanks to Nicole Eisenman for being a generous "genius."

To the great Cristina Miranda, for generously giving her time and expertise to scanning drawings.

To Carol Calhoun for the quiet retreat by the water where this book was completed and for being the perfect reader.

To Sarah Funke Butler for believing that this book has an audience and for representing the project with such enthusiasm. Thanks for getting it out in the world.

To Patty Rice at Andrews McMeel for taking this on and for being such a pleasure to work with.

To David Colagiovanni for his infectious giggles and for the website help.

To Michael Medieros at The Emily Dickinson Museum for sharing his knowledge of interesting "facts" about the poet.

To Justine Jablonska and Rachel Beach for "The Slanted Life... The Movie."

To Chrissy and Paul Wasserman for lots of stuff.

And to Patrizia Cavalli for the gift of her live renditions of Emily's poems, and to Angela Dufresne for providing the circumstance.

To Julia Elsas for last-minute Photoshopping and other stuff.

THE Slanted LIFE of Emily Dickinson

Andrews McMeel Publishing
a division of Andrews McMeel Universal
1130 Walnut Street, Kansas City, Missouri 64106

www.andrewsmcmeel.com

17 18 19 20 21 RR2 10 9 8 7 6 5 4 3 2 1

ISBN: 978-1-4494-8135-3

Library of Congress Control Number: 2016949503

Editor: Patty Rice
Designer/Art Director: Diane Marsh
Production Manager: Cliff Koehler
Production Editor: Erika Kuster

ATTENTION: SCHOOLS AND BUSINESSES

Andrews McMeel books are available at quantity discounts with bulk purchase for educational, business, or sales promotional use. For information, please e-mail the Andrews McMeel Publishing Special Sales Department: specialsales@amuniversal.com.